SHORT CU

INTRODUCTIONS TO FILM STUDIES

OTHER TITLES IN THE SHORT CUTS SERIES

SILENT CINEMA

BEFORE THE PICTURES GOT SMALL

LAWRENCE NAPPER

WALLFLOWER

LONDON and NEW YORK

A Wallflower Press Book
Published by
Columbia University Press
Publishers Since 1893
New York • Chichester, West Sussex
cup.columbia.edu

A complete CIP record is available from the Library of Congress

ISBN 978-0-231-18118-1 (cloth : alk. paper)
ISBN 978-0-231-18117-4 (pbk. : alk. paper)
ISBN 978-0-231-54350-7 (e-book)

Columbia University Press books are printed on permanent and durable acid-free paper.
Printed in the United States of America

Cover image: ASPHALT (1929) © Universum Film (UFA)

CONTENTS

ACKNOWLEDGEMENTS

Thanks to fellow fans and scholars of silent cinema who have taught, and taught with me over the years: Charles Barr, Tim Bergfelder, Jane Bryan, Jon Burrows, Pam Cook, Bryony Dixon, Richard Dyer, Pier Ercole, Tony Fletcher, Mark Fuller, Christine Gledhill, Elena Gorfinkel, Hannah Hamad, Mike Hammond, Andrew Higson, Pamela Hutchinson, Kristian Moen, Stephen Morgan, Kulraj Phullar, Laraine Porter, Sue Porter, Eleonora Sammartino, Amy Sargeant, Alison Strauss, Clare Watson, Michael Williams.

Thanks to friends and family who have supported me while writing, particularly Adrian and Paula Napper, Sheri Conklin, Mark Jeanes and Simon Greenacre.

This book is dedicated to the musicians who make silent films come alive, particularly to: Neil Brand, Guenter Buchwald, Philip Carli, Cyrus Gabrysch, Jane Gardner, Lillian Henley, Stephen Horne, John Sweeney.

INTRODUCTION

'We didn't need dialogue. We had faces!'

This defiant statement by Norma Desmond (Gloria Swanson) in *Sunset Boulevard* (Billy Wilder, 1950) strives to correct a key misunderstanding about silent cinema that still prevails today – that it is characterised by *lack*. The very category 'silent cinema' defines filmmaking before 1926 not on its own terms, but against a later and apparently more complete 'sound cinema'. In its heyday, however, silent cinema was never understood to 'lack' sound. Silent films were typically accompanied by live music, of course, but it was more than that. Before synchronised sound technology was introduced, 'silent cinema' didn't even exist as a category. It was simply 'cinema', complete in itself – the most modern, most popular, most eloquent, most glamorous mass-communication medium of its day.

Even before he meets her, Joe Gillis (William Holden) identifies Norma as belonging to a lost age. Her house is a 'white elephant', the kind of place he would expect to find a Miss Haversham-style figure, 'taking it out on the world, because she'd been given the go-by'. Norma, of course, turns out to be exactly such a figure. Hopelessly stuck in the past, her affiliation with silent cinema marks her out as both tragic and sinister, and her refusal to admit the superiority of sound is a kind of mad delusion that can only end in death. Typically for a film noir, this obsession is linked to her sexuality. The film draws a parallel between Norma's inappropriate allegiance to a lost cinematic form and her 'inappropriate' desire for Joe. Both are presented to the audience as taboo and disgusting because they persist long after their time has past. Students are often reluctant to read the relationship between Joe and Norma as consummated, but despite its misogyny, *Sunset Boulevard* hinges on this paradox. Norma is attractive despite her antiquity. She is still – as she was in her heyday – charismatic, potent, fascinating and *sexy*.

I have chosen to open with a discussion of *Sunset Boulevard* because, unlike even the most famous examples of actual silent cinema, it is likely to be familiar to most general readers. Indeed, many people's understanding of silent film is gleaned from a combination of this film and *Singin' in the Rain* (Stanley Donen, 1952), another narrative that insists on silent cinema as characterised by lack. Fending off the amorous advances of Don Lockwood (Gene Kelly), Kathy Selden (Debbie Reynolds) identifies silent movies as 'entertaining enough for the masses', but draws an unflattering analogy with the art of the theatre: 'The personalities on the screen just don't impress me. I mean they don't talk, they don't act. They just make a lot of dumb show. Well, you know ... like that!' In the ellipsis she produces a remarkably economic pastiche of melodramatic acting, using stock gestures to convey desire, horror and surprise in quick succession. It is a brilliant moment, which deftly creates a particular idea of silent cinema in the audience's mind. The gestural acting imitated by Kathy is in a tradition that early films inherited from the Victorian stage melodrama. It survived into the cinema of the 1910s, but by the late 1920s (when *Singin' in the Rain* is set) it had certainly been superseded by a more naturalistic and restrained style of screen performance. Nevertheless, like Norma Desmond's artificial mannerisms, Kathy's 'dumb show' emphasises the un-naturalness of a medium apparently struggling to compensate for the 'lack' of sound.

Sunset Boulevard and *Singin' in the Rain* are now over sixty years old, and yet they still circulate widely in contemporary popular culture. They are often cited in lists of favourite films compiled by people of all ages. They are regularly re-shown on television, often scheduled as highlights of holiday viewing. They have both been adapted into stage musicals, and revivals of both have enjoyed successful London West End runs in recent years. Despite their age, then, these films appear able to reach across the years and 'speak' to modern viewers, who interpret their aesthetic and generic codes with relative ease. By contrast, only twenty years separates the release of these films and the decline of the silent cinema that they dramatise. While both films celebrate that cinema, they also insist on its technological and aesthetic obsolescence in comparison to sound cinema. Norma Desmond's greatest cinematic successes are presented purely as aesthetic curiosities, relics of a bygone age – like their star. 'The Duelling Cavalier' is gently mocked as a crude and childish entertainment, suggestive of more unsophisticated times. According to these films an unbridgeable gulf seems to exist between silent and sound cinema, one which renders all films made before the introduction of sound ridiculous to modern audiences – their alien and antique style a source of embarrassment and incomprehension, rather than pleasure and enjoyment. Such ideas were nothing new. As early as 1937 when the modern young heroine of the British film *Gangway* (Sonnie Hale, 1937) is given the task of shadowing a film star suspected of a jewelry theft, she complains that the star was 'only good in silent pictures. Her bones creek!'

That sense of silent cinema as somehow separated from the rest of film culture is one that still prevails today, despite a recent resurgence of interest in the form. Screenings of silent films on television are still relatively rare. Many university film studies courses either ignore silent films altogether, or annex them in a single module designed to cover the whole of cinema up to 1930. Aside from specialist festivals, silent films are rarely programmed in repertory cinemas, or when they are, the titles are selected from a relatively narrow range of known 'classics'. The ubiquity of titles such as *The Cabinet of Dr Caligari* (Robert Weine, 1920) and *Battleship Potemkin* (Sergei Eisenstein, 1925) in such revivals, tend to reinforce the idea that only iconic *avant garde* masterworks have the ability to transcend the 'handicap' of silence, and speak directly to modern audiences.

It is the aim of this book to challenge that notion. By outlining the historical contexts of their production, and suggesting some interpretative frameworks through which they might be approached, I hope to enable readers to experience these films not as technical or artistic curiosities, but as emotionally fulfilling, pleasurable entertainments in their own right – as audiences of the 1920s experienced them.

The focus will be on late silent cinema – roughly from the First World War onwards.[1]

In Chapter One I shall consider the cinema of the 1920s from the point of view of those who went to see it. What was it that attracted people to the cinema, and what was their experience when they got there? How were the images and ideas people encountered in the cinema incorporated into their daily lives? Here I will draw on the ways in which cinema-going was actually represented *within* a range of films from the silent period, teasing out what can be gleaned from the films themselves about the experiences of their audiences.

The cinemas of Weimar Germany and Soviet Russia are often acknowledged to be the most distinctive and influential in the Europe of the 1920s. Indeed, 'Soviet montage' and 'German expressionism' are perhaps the two phrases most closely associated with silent cinema. Both countries experienced cataclysmic social and political upheavals as a result of the First World War, and their distinctive cinematic styles are often understood to emerge from those upheavals, offering politically charged alternatives to the dominant Hollywood style, either consciously (in the case of Soviet Russia) or somehow subconsciously (in the case of Germany). Both styles were seized on by serious critics in the period as evidence of cinema's potential as great 'Art', and have remained central to intellectual approaches to film culture ever since.

Chapters Two and Three respectively will examine these claims with regard to German expressionist and Soviet montage films, considering some of the most famous examples such as *The Cabinet of Dr Caligari* and *Battleship Potemkin*. However, despite the impression given in many accounts, the mass film-going publics of Germany and Russia didn't subsist on *avant garde* masterworks alone. Some of the more conventional popular genres will be considered as well, and discussions of films such as *The Oyster Princess* (Ernst Lubitsch, 1919) and *The Girl With the Hatbox* (Boris Barnet, 1927) will demonstrate both the liveliness and variety of popular film cultures of continental Europe. Here, I suggest, we will see an interest in working through themes to do with modernity, consumerism and gender relations within a framework of entertaining narrative, genre and romance.

Chapter Four will consider the most important cinema of the age — Hollywood. What were the factors that enabled American filmmakers to establish such dominance in the world cinema market, and how did their films represent this quintessentially modern nation to itself and the world? *It* (Clarence Badger, 1927) offers an opportunity to consider the way in which crucial questions of modernity, mass consumerism and shifting gender relations were worked through within an overall cinematic system that emphasised the pleasures of narrative, romance and genre.

Chapter Five will consider perhaps the most derided European cinema of the period: the British cinema. Caught between the populism of Hollywood and the 'Art' of Europe, British cinema of the 1920s enjoyed a dolorous reputation among both the film intellectuals of the period (who considered it insignificant compared to the art cinemas of Europe), and commercial commentators (who considered it amateurish compared to Hollywood). Its most famous director, Alfred Hitchcock, made no effort to enhance its reputation with posterity, preferring to create the impression that he was a lone talent in a desert of mediocrity. However, recent scholars have looked again at the films produced in Britain in the 1920s and discovered a rich and varied collection of work, emerging from a vibrant and fascinating industry.

'I am big. It's the pictures that got small.'

Before we move on though, it may be useful first to consider why it was that the films of the silent era were so quickly forgotten after 1930. Common sense might suggest that a fundamental shift in the aesthetics of cinema might be the explanation. The introduction of sound, one might imagine, represented such a 'quantum leap' in the ability of cinema to represent reality that the artificiality of silent techniques were immediately exposed and rendered laughable. In fact the truth is very different. While the introduction of sound did involve some aesthetic shifts, it didn't alter the fundamentals of cinematic language, which had become standard by around 1917. In fact, techniques of editing and framing remained remarkably consistent across the transition to sound (see Crafton 1999: 5). A range of other factors to do with technology, economics and cultural attitudes can be understood as just as important to the creation of the 'gulf' between silent and sound.

'You're Norma Desmond! You used to be in pictures. You used to be big!' exclaims Joe Gillis when he first recognises Norma. 'I *am* big,' is her defiant response, 'it's the *pictures* that got small.' Technically, Norma's claim that 'the pictures got small' is absolutely right. During the silent period the space inside the sprocket holes of a standard 35mm strip of film was entirely filled with the picture being projected. After the introduction of sound, some of that picture space had to be given up to make way for the soundtrack, which ran in a narrow strip down the side of the film between the sprocket holes and the image. Furthermore, in order to maintain the standard proportions of the image as projected on the screen, the space lost at the side of the image was matched by space at the top of the image. Audiences watching a sound film wouldn't be aware of these changes. A metal plate was introduced into the projector to mask the soundtrack so it wasn't visible on the screen. But if a silent film was projected through a sound projector, the side and the top of the image was obscured, giving the impression that early filmmakers consistently chopped their characters' heads off and failed to capture action occurring on the left of the screen. This wasn't the only humiliation silent films suffered in the age of sound. While projection speeds in the silent era had varied between 16 and 24 frames per second (fps), sound technology demanded an absolutely consistent projection speed of 24fps. Thus silent films projected on sound technology were always speeded up. 'Headless' characters ran around the screen at a chaotic and comedic pace, even in films that weren't comedies – a characteristic that we still associate with silent film even today.

Economic factors also militated against the continued reputation and circulation of silent cinema. Sound film represented a massive investment in research and development for those studios that had thrown their weight behind it, and yet the inevitability of its triumph was not evident at the time. Cinema managers were initially resistant – not surprisingly given the expense that converting cinemas to sound involved, and the rather inconsistent quality of the earliest sound films. *The Jazz Singer* (Alan Crosland, 1927) is generally understood to be the big breakthrough for sound. It was released as a sound film in the US in 1927, but UK audiences and audiences away from the big cities in America only saw it in a silent version. In fact it wasn't until as late as 1931 that the transition to sound film was complete in the US and the UK. In countries where Hollywood films didn't dominate the cinemas, the transition took even longer – Japan did not turn to sound until the mid-1930s. This long and uncertain period of transition suggests that sound wasn't spontaneously adopted by audiences as a self-evidently superior form of cinema. Instead it had to be consistently *promoted* by the production companies who had invested so much in it (much as 3D technology is promoted today). Part of that promotion strategy involved deliberately creating the impression of a gulf dividing the modern 'talkies' with the antiquated silent films. As Donald Crafton suggests, 'the promoters of sound represented their devices as a total break with the past' (1999: 4). In this project they were assisted by a further economic factor: film was both expensive to keep (being both bulky and inflammable) and had a high scrap value (due to its silver content). Many producers found it more economic to sell their old films for scrap rather than spend money on warehousing and fire insurance costs in anticipation of them being useful later. As a result, a large proportion of silent film titles never actually survived into the sound period, and many more were lost in the years after 1930. Many of the films that did survive, did so only as a result of the amateur home movie market, where they were re-released in cut-down versions – literally in versions which were printed on physically smaller stock (on amateur gauges such as 16mm or 9.5mm), and had been edited into shorter running times to suit the needs of home projection shows. When silent films *were* seen after 1930, then, it was often only in diminished versions of themselves.

Finally, a range of cultural factors also weighed against the continuing presence of silent films after 1930. Today we are surrounded by old films – on television, on DVD, on YouTube and Netflix. We think nothing of settling down to watch a film released last year, five years ago, or perhaps even sixty years ago. This longevity of individual films has its origins in the growth of television in the 1950s, which regularly scheduled older films both as 'event' programming and as 'filler'. Later, home entertainment systems such as VHS and DVD made re-watching films even easier. Before television, though, films had very little life after their initial cinematic release. Some blockbusters such as *The Four Horsemen of the Apocalypse* (Rex Ingram, 1921), or *Ben-Hur* (Fred Niblo, 1925), or popular series such as the Charlie Chaplin comedies might have enjoyed a cinematic re-release after a few years. Some commercial cinemas in places like central London regularly revived films deemed to be 'classics'. Nevertheless, the vast majority of films vanished after their initial cinematic run, and film fans wouldn't expect to see them again – ever. Films were understood, both by fans and by the industry itself, to be essentially ephemeral objects. As a result, audience taste moved more rapidly than we are used to today, and films only a few years old were quickly thought to have dated. When television did start to re-introduce audiences to older films from the 1950s onwards, silent films were 'given the go-by' due to understandable cost considerations – broadcasting a silent film involved the extra trouble and expense of adding a musical score – it was easier to leave them alone and concentrate on post-1930 productions.

Sometimes, though, history is kind. More recent technological developments have worked in favour of, rather than against, silent cinema. Digital restoration techniques have allowed many more films to become visible than in previous years, and for those films to be presented more sympathetically. Archivists and restorers have been able to ensure that films which were previously too fragile to be shown, can now be presented looking as pristine and perfect as they looked on their first release. The internet has meant that many such restorations are now freely available to download, or to watch, and the increased interest in screening events with live musical performance mean that its more possible to see such films on the big screen. There's never been a better time to be a fan of silent cinema. This book will help you get started.

Note

1   For an account of filmmaking up to 1914, see S. Popple and J. Kember (2003) *Early Cinema: From Factory Gate to Dream Palace*. London: Wallflower Press.

1   GOING TO THE PICTURES

'You can't go out again, you must stay home. You waste your money
on that common Picturedrome.'
                              – Noel Coward, 'Mad About the Boy' (1932)

Who went to the cinema in the 1920s? How regularly did they go, and what
were the cinemas they went to like? How did they relate to the films they
saw? How did their experiences at the cinema affect their view of the world
and their place within it?

Some of the answers to these questions can be found in the films
themselves, which from the beginning frequently depicted characters
'going to the pictures'. In Robert W. Paul's *The Countryman and the
Cinematograph* (1901), a rural worker is shown experiencing the cinema
for the first time. He is highly amused by a film of dancing girls and imitates
their dance moves in front of the screen. A film of a train coming towards
the camera alarms him, and he 'runs away' from it, re-enacting a popular
contemporary anecdote about naive viewers being unable to distinguish
between moving pictures and reality. But he is not scared for long, and is
drawn back to the screen by images of a countryman like himself flirting
with a pretty woman. As it survives, the film is less than twenty seconds
long, but in that short time it manages to demonstrate cinema's ability
to provoke laugher, fear and erotic attraction, as well as suggesting the
power of 'identification' – of watching cinematic versions of oneself. Most

Fig. 1: *Those Awful Hats* (1909); inside a nickelodeon.

importantly though, it envisages the countryman's encounter with cinema as an encounter with *modernity*.[1] What remains of Paul's film shows few details of the screening space – a decorated proscenium suggests the film is being shown in a music-hall as part of a mixed programme (as was common in the 1900s), or perhaps the elaborately decorated interior of a travelling fairground cinematograph show.

D. W. Griffith's *Those Awful Hats* (1909) illustrates how films were exhibited a decade later, after the development of fixed-site cinemas. Such early venues were known as 'nickelodeons' in the US and they sprung up rapidly in towns and cities from 1905 onwards. Most were small venues, perhaps converted shops, holding no more than a hundred people. In Griffith's film, the audience sit on bentwood chairs that have been arranged in rows but are not fixed to the ground. A screen onto which the films are projected hangs against the end wall of the auditorium and to the side of the screen a single pianist provides accompaniment on an upright piano. He and the screen are separated from the audience by a wooden railing. Initially the predominantly male audience appear absorbed in the film – they point to the screen and comment to each other on what is going on there.

At one point, when the hero embraces the heroine, they applaud. However, they do not remain focused on the screen for long. A garishly dressed man in a top hat, accompanied by a be-hatted lady-friend appear, and make so much fuss trying to find seats that an altercation ensues.

Later a whole stream of ladies enter, wearing enormous 'matinee' hats piled high with ornamental fruit and feathers. They sit in the front row, blocking everyone's view of the screen. Pandemonium ensues. At the height of the chaos a giant jaw descends from the ceiling and carries one of the ladies' hats off. All but one of the others hastily remove their hats for fear of a similar fate. The diehard hat-wearer stands and remonstrates with the audience until the jaw returns and carries her off completely. The film ends with a slightly less emphatic attempt to police audience behaviour – an inter-title requesting ladies to 'Please remove their hats!'

This attempt to ensure decorum in the auditorium is a reflection of the increasing desire throughout the nickelodeon period for 'uplift'. Cinema's early reputation as a primarily working-class entertainment, the *frisson* associated with men and women sitting un-chaperoned together in the dark and the popularity of films with children and adolescents all combined to give picture-going a rather disreputable flavour. Cinema attracted the attention of moral and religious reformers who characterised the nickelodeons as the resort of 'mashers' and as a training ground for vice and criminality among the young who, they claimed, were seduced into lives of crime by the stories they saw on the screen. 'Uplift' was the industry's attempt to combat this reputation, and to shift the appeal of cinema towards the more respectable (and lucrative) middle-class market. Ambitious managers strove to attract such audiences by emphasising the respectability of their houses as demonstrated by their well-appointed facilities and the decorum of their audiences. In the UK, the Cinematograph Act of 1909 further changed the character of the cinema auditorium. Primarily a fire safety measure, it stipulated that cinemas could only gain a licence to operate if they were built to strict specifications – with the projector enclosed in a separate room, and with adequate fire escapes and circulation spaces. The small converted shop-front cinema was giving way to larger purpose-built venues. From 1909 in the US and from 1912 in the UK, production companies also took action to combat accusations from moral reformers. They co-operated to form independent boards of censorship, which vetted every film released to ensure a consistent moral standard. Scholars have suggested a parallel between the drive for 'uplift' and developments in narrative style and psychological realism that occurred in this period, particularly in American cinema (see Gunning 2003: 148). Representations of crime and vice were not banned outright, but they were contained within overall narratives that emphasised either retribution or moral transformation for their protagonists. Murderers were hanged. Sinners repented.

Concerns about the moral influence of cinema didn't completely disappear, of course. Evidence suggests that anxiety about improper sexual activity in the auditorium increased in the early war years, as did the policing of such activity (see Sanders 2002: 97). Nevertheless, during the First World War a number of high-profile and extremely successful feature films established the importance of cinema both as a serious medium and as an art form. In Britain, *The Battle of the Somme* (Geoffrey Malins & John McDowell, 1916) enabled audiences to make sense of their loved ones' experiences at the front. An 'official' filmed record of the war, it was astonishingly popular at the box office, and widely discussed in even the most respectable newspapers. The Italian epic *Cabiria* (Giovanni Pastroni, 1914) and the American film *The Birth of a Nation* (D. W. Griffith, 1915) were also instrumental in raising the profile of cinema, and enabling it to shed some of its early associations with cheap entertainment. Epic both in conception and in duration, these films demanded special treatment. *The Birth of a Nation* was shown in London's premiere theatrical venue (The Theatre Royal, Drury Lane), and ticket prices were commensurate with those of a West End show. They are also indicative a wider shift from the 15–20-minute running times of the feature productions shown in the nickelodeon period, towards the more familiar standard 90-minute feature we still have today.

Certainly by 1917 middle-class patrons could frequent the cinema with no suggestion of impropriety. In *Wild and Woolly* (John Emerson, 1917), Douglas Fairbanks plays Jeff Hillington, the son of a wealthy railroad magnet living in New York City, and a regular cinemagoer. His passion for films is just one part of a wider passion for the Wild West, which he also indulges through popular prints and dime novels. Nevertheless it is the cinema where, as an inter-title tells us, 'his dreams come true' and where he returns every week for relief from the tedious grind of clerical work in his father's office. We see him approaching the street pay-box of a downtown cinema, which is festooned with posters for the westerns that became popular around 1909 and which remained a staple of American cinema thereafter. *Wild and Woolly* is itself a sort of self-conscious western, for while Jeff is 'revelling in his picture-play West' the film transports the audience to the 'real' West – which is rather more modern than Jeff's cinema-inspired fantasy. Instead of the honest challenge of the wide-open prairies, 'Bitter Creek, Arizona' is a place of government and business corruption. The film, then, gently mocks Jeff's cinema habit, suggesting that his enthusiastic and wholesale acceptance of cinema's simplistic version of the West marks him out as rather infantile. Nevertheless, when he is himself transported to Arizona, it is the values of 'the West' that he has learnt in the picture house – of boyish enthusiasm, honest dealing, physical agility and moral absolutism – that save the day and win him the girl of his dreams. The anxieties of moral reformers are here turned on their heads – cinema may indeed be an influence on impressionable young people, but here it is offered as an influence for the good – a force to mould them into moral upright American citizens (see Studlar 1996: 10–90).

It was not just in America that filmmakers were concerned to portray cinema as a benevolent moral force. The Italian film *Maciste* (Luigi Bor-gnetto & Vincenzo Denizot, 1915) offers cinema as a space of safety both physically and intellectually. When it opens, the un-named heroine (Clementina Gay) is fleeing her enemies. From the dark and deserted suburbs she heads for the main streets and the crowded Cinema Excelsior, which offers safety in numbers, packed as it is for a screening of the smash-hit *Cabiria*. We are shown the interior of the cinema, which is very much in the style of a stage theatre. There is a proscenium, and stage boxes, elaborate decorative plasterwork and curtains, and rows of fixed seating fill the stalls. As is appropriate for a film of *Cabiria*'s stature, the screening is accompanied by a full pit orchestra, complete with conductor. Outside the cinema there is a uniformed doorman distributing flyers. The heroine enters the auditorium just as *Cabiria*'s star, the heroic strong-man slave Maciste (Bartolomeo Pagano) is shown escaping a dungeon by breaking through its iron bars with his bare hands. The audience are vocal in their approval, applauding and gesturing to the thrilling climax unfolding on the screen. The heroine stands behind some respectably dressed women who are transfixed by the drama, and she herself forgets her troubles in the face of the spectacle. Later, in a brilliantly self-reflexive move, she writes to Maciste (care of the film studios) asking for his protection in real life and declaring her hope that his 'bravery and goodness are not just screen fiction'.

Maciste offers a particularly satisfying early demonstration of the contours of film stardom and the complexity of the relationship between the cinema star and his or her fans. Pagano (the actor) and Maciste (the character) are conflated so that, while understanding that the Maciste of *Cabiria* is a fiction, the heroine still writes to the character, rather than to the actor personifying him – and the film of course makes the same elision. Pagano went on to star as Maciste a further 25 times between 1916 and 1927, and his image became so associated with virtuous Italian masculinity that Mussolini is said to have modelled himself on the character (see Reich 2015: 187).

In *Sherlock Jnr* (Buster Keaton, 1924) Buster Keaton plays a projectionist in a small-town cinema who also comes to model himself on the characters onscreen. The cinema shown here is substantially changed from the one in *Those Awful Hats*. It is larger – purpose built, with fixed seating arranged in rows and a central aisle. Prominently marked exit doors are positioned on either side of the screen. There is still a railing separating the audience from the screen, but the pianist is joined by several other musicians, making up a small ensemble to accompany the film. At one point the dreaming projectionist actually projects himself *into* the film, leaping over the pianist to enter the screen and remonstrate with a villain who he takes to be seducing his sweetheart. In the final moments of the film, when he has woken to find himself back in the projection box, with his sweetheart alongside him and the obstacles of the plot all cleared away, he literally takes his cue from the final moments of the film he is projecting in order to overcome his shyness with regard to her. As the hero onscreen takes his lover's hands and kisses them, so the projectionist does the same. When she looks away modestly, he checks the screen again to see the cinema hero's next move – extracting a ring from his pocket and putting it on her finger; the projectionist does the same. The relationship between cinema and courtship is also put to comic effect in *The Patsy* (King Vidor, 1928) when Patricia (Marion Davis), trying to get the attention of a boy, adopts a series of different feminine guises in imitation of famous film stars of the period. Respectively she pretends to be the party girl (Mae Marsh), the modest maid (Lillian Gish) and the exotic vamp (Pola Negri).

From *The Countryman and the Cinematograph* onwards, then, these images of film-going give a sense not only of how the experience of 'going to the cinema' changed from the turn of the century to the 1920s, but also of the role cinema was understood to play in the lives of film-goers. In each of these examples, watching films is understood not just as an innocuous way of passing one's leisure hours, but as something more than that – a way of understanding and thinking about the world and one's place within it. The countryman's simple imitation of the dancers he sees onscreen in 1901, and his later identification with the man dressed like him on screen, has become a much more complex process. For Jeff in *Wild and Woolly* it has helped to form his ideas about what it means to be an American; for the hero of *Sherlock Jnr.* it provides a model for how to behave towards a girl; while for Patricia in *The Patsy* it provides a series of models of how to *be* a girl (albeit models that are gently mocked). The heroine of *Maciste*'s engagement with the charismatic star persona of that film is perhaps more complex – he represents an ideal of masculinity to which she responds (and which is also intertwined with ideas of Italian-ness). Her response is typical of film fans even today – she seeks to bridge the gap between herself and the star (or perhaps between 'ordinary' life and the 'thrill' of cinema) by writing to him.

It is perhaps not surprising that each of these films represents the influence of the cinema as broadly benign, since they were produced by the film industry itself. Nevertheless, more ambivalent portrayals can also be found. *Bed and Sofa* (Abram Room, 1927) was produced in the USSR and concerns three young Russians – a wife, a husband and the husband's old army friend – who are forced to share a cramped one-room apartment. Early indications suggest that the three are a little bit more committed to bourgeois notions of personal desire and private fulfilment than is ideal in the new Soviet society. The husband, Kolia (Nikolai Batalov), would rather rush straight home than attend a party meeting after work. Their flat is cluttered with trivial decorative knick knacks, and the wife, Luidia (Lyudmila Semyonova), reads film magazines. When Kolia has to go away for work, his friend Volodia (Vladimir Fogel) takes Luidia out for the day. They end up in the cinema together. The scene is extremely brief. A rather spartan hall with what looks like a temporary screen, they sit on hard chairs and Luidia exclaims how long it is since she went to the pictures as the lights dim. Nevertheless, the scene is set, and when they return home Volodia makes a pass at her and she accepts. Their night together initiates the *ménage a trois* arrangement which is the film's theme. To modern eyes, the film's matter-of-fact treatment of the situation seems astonishing. When Kolia returns, his nose is briefly put out of joint, but he accepts the situation, which continues until Volodia starts mistreating Luidia, at which point she transfers her affections back to her husband. Finally, she gets sick of them both, and when neither of them seem prepared to take responsibility for her pregnancy, she books an appointment for an abortion, but changes her mind at the last minute and simply leaves the two men to fend for themselves and moves to another town. Despite (or perhaps because of) the film's un-sensational treatment, it sparked considerable debate and controversy in the USSR on its release, both for its attempt to show questions of everyday life and for its refusal to resolve those questions. Julian Gaffy describes the widespread discussion of the film, not just in cinema journals and newspapers, but in factory cinema clubs and at union meetings (precisely the sort of meetings that Kolia in the film declines to attend). He quotes the film's director Abram Room, arguing for the film as a '*problem* film', one which 'besides the normal tasks of capturing daily life … also poses certain problem tasks, touches a certain question of how we construct our daily life'. With this explicit function of cinema in mind, Room celebrated the fact that his film was everywhere 'accompanied by special showings, discussions, questionnaires, collective reviews and so on…' (2001: 100). Two different ideas about cinema are counterpoised in *Bed and Sofa*, then. On the one hand, film-going is shown within the film is as a slightly decadent habit – a source of daydreaming and erotic surrender; on the other, Room's model of the film itself is as a tool to actively provoke debate among its audiences about the social and moral values of the new Soviet society.

My final example comes from the now celebrated sequence in the British film *A Cottage on Dartmoor* (Anthony Asquith, 1929). It was made at the very end of the silent period, and although it is a silent film, it shows people going to a cinema that has recently been converted to show the new 'talkies' as part of its programme. Joe (Uno Henning), a rather shy barber, is sweet on Sally (Norah Baring), a manicurist who also works in the same shop. He has bought tickets to the 'talkies' and asks her to accompany him after work. She peremptorily refuses, leaving him crest-fallen. The invitation to the cinema, of course, was merely a pretext and this is made clear when another girl, eyeing Joe and his tickets, declares '*I'm* terribly fond of the pictures!' Joe completely fails to take the hint. For the girl, a trip to the pictures combines the pleasure of the film show and the pleasure of sitting in the dark next to a nice-looking boy. Joe, it seems, is not a film fan, and for him the cinema is merely an excuse to get close to one specific girl – Sally. As time goes on Sally strikes up a relationship with another man, Harry (Hans Schlettow). But Joe is unable to move on from his obsession with her. When Harry takes Sally to the pictures, Joe's obsession is such that he follows them jealously, and observes their date from a seat a little way off. The sequence is longer and more complex than any of those discussed above, and unlike most of those examples it contains no wide shot of the auditorium, or image of the screen. The sense of the film-going experience is made up entirely of close-ups of the various audience members in the dim light of the auditorium, and of the orchestra. We know that they are sitting in the balcony of the cinema, and the seating is quite heavily raked. Sally and Harry sit down, and we see the variety of other cinema-goers around them as they watch a Harold Lloyd comedy before the main feature. Sally politely takes off her hat when the middle-aged woman behind her requests, although the same woman refuses to take her own hat off when asked by the lady behind *her*. The musicians are working hard with the film – they are a medium-sized ensemble, a pianist, drummer, trombonist and two violins. They play an up-tempo number to accompany the slapstick that we must assume is proceeding on screen.

There are many reasons for going to the cinema besides romance, it seems, and the sequence offers us some of them. One middle-aged man looks bored with the film, and later falls fast asleep, enjoying an evening in the warmth and darkness of the cinema that perhaps he can't get at home. Two schoolboys, chomping on their toffees, are completely engrossed in the comedy, until to their confusion and excitement they notice that the man sitting next to them uncannily resembles Harold Lloyd himself. Most people respond to the comedy by laughing, and we see the laughter of the lady with the hat, the elderly lady next to her, a thin spinsterish lady, a middle-aged swell sporting a monocle, as well as that of the schoolboys and of Sally. The film, cutting between close-ups of each of these characters, suggests cinema as an inclusive, communal experience. Nevertheless, individual pre-occupations are still delineated among the crowd. Sally is intent on the film, her expression anticipating some of the gags, and then smiling and laughing with relief when visual punch-lines come. Harry, sitting next to her, spends some of his time gazing at her as she watches the screen. Joe, behind them, takes no notice of the film at all, intent as he is on monitoring the body language between 'his' girl and his rival. When the 'talkie' comes on we see the musicians put down their instruments and take a well-earned break. They pass glasses of beer among them and munch on sandwiches, smoke, and later play cards. Their disinterest in the film suggests their familiarity with it, but is also a reminder that cinema isn't about leisure for everyone. For the musicians it is a site of paid labour. The silent comedy had meant hard work. The talkie, by contrast, means enforced idleness for the present, and probably redundancy in the not-too-distant future.

The talkie is evidently not a comedy, but a drama of suspense. For the old woman next to the lady with the hat the new technology creates its own problems. She draws an ear trumpet from her bag, and requires her neighbour to repeat the screen dialogue into it, much to the irritation of those around them. The sequence very clearly suggests that the talkies require a new habit of silence in the cinema auditorium. On three separate occasions a climax in the drama leads a different audience member to applaud enthusiastically – much as we saw the audiences in *Those Awful Hats* and *Maciste* applauding. Here, though, the applause is quickly checked by each person's companion as though it is an embarrassing outburst. Nevertheless, the emotional trajectory of the drama is clearly indicated by the physical reactions of the audience – and in some cases, it provides them with a justification for the other pleasures of which they may have come to the auditorium in search. As the drama becomes increasingly tense, so most audience members lean forward in their seats, engrossed in the action. The tension doesn't stop one man checking his watch, realising

Fig. 2: *A Cottage on Dartmoor* (1929); suspenseful action onscreen encourages intimacy in the auditorium.

he's missed an appointment and leaving, and it doesn't affect the man who is fast asleep. But for the others, the heightened psychological involvement in the screen has a physical affect. Sally and Harry lean forward, moving together as they do so. The two schoolboys, their eyes widening, similarly move forward, as does Joe (although from different motives – he is jealously watching the couple rather than the screen). Sally reaches out for Harry's arm, and Harry, who has been admiring her as much as watching the screen hitherto, also begins to concentrate on the drama.

Eventually their temples are touching as they watch together. This romantic pairing is matched by that of another couple, whose relationship seems rather more casual. At the start of the scene they lean apart, clearly indicating that they are strangers. A minor revelation in the drama gives them an excuse to exchange knowing glances, and immediately having sized each other up, they shift position leaning closer together across their shared armrest. Later we see her engrossed while he looks across, notices her absorption and smiles to himself. Their shoulders are definitely touching now. Later still, in the moment of maximum tension in the onscreen drama she (perhaps) unconsciously reaches for his arm and he immediately responds, placing his hand on hers. The contract is complete. Moral reformers of the 1910s would have had plenty to say about the audience in this cinema! Sally and Harry may be on a genuine date, affirming their growing love for each other through the shared pleasure of watching a film drama. But one could argue that the other couple are involved in a decidedly more *louche* activity – they came into the cinema auditorium seeking a casual thrill greater than that offered on the screen.

Meanwhile, Joe is a more sinister figure still. Using the semi-private/semi-public space of the darkened auditorium to observe without being observed, he is effectively stalking Sally. While the other characters gaze at the screen and react to what they see there, Joe never takes his eyes off Sally. He seems utterly unaware of the film playing before him. He is thinking about something completely different, and in fact we are shown what is passing through his mind's eye. It is *A Cottage on Dartmoor* itself as we have watched it so far, in the form of flashbacks of the previous scenes delineating his failed courtship of Sally and his impotent observation of her growing intimacy with Harry. The fact that the film gives us this privileged information into what Joe is thinking suggests that on some level we are expected to empathise with him or identify with him in some way.

He is indeed the main character whose emotions we follow most consistently throughout the narrative. We know more about his experiences, his desires and his motivations than we do about any of the other characters. And yet we could hardly call him the 'hero' of the film in the usual positive sense of that term (suggesting the character we relate to, feel is similar to us, and that we emulate). His behaviour towards Sally is creepy and obsessive by this point, and will continue to be so as the film develops. *A Cottage on Dartmoor* takes to extreme the ambivalence we felt towards the Countryman in *The Countryman and the Cinematograph*; the suspicion that Jeff in *Wild and Woolly* was a bit of a bully; the moral ambiguity of the characters in *Bed and Sofa*. In its portrayal of the audience at the cinema, the film offers a range of possibilities of how audiences might relate to a story onscreen, and also to the cinema auditorium in which they view that story. Throughout the sequence, something quite scary has evidently been unfolding in the film the characters are watching – they react as though they are in sympathy with a character in peril, although the film itself invites us to be in sympathy both with Sally (who is in peril) and with Joe (who is the source of her peril), not to mention a variety of other characters with completely different concerns.

At the climax of the 'talkie', a frightening event occurs onscreen and some of the audience instinctively turn away – unable to watch. One woman screws her eyes shut, and Sally buries her face in Harry's shoulder. The schoolboys, on the other hand, are delighted, and applaud, while the sleeping man remains utterly oblivious. In the relief straight after this moment of climax, Sally and Harry look lovingly at each other, and the other couple also exchange a glance, openly leaning together while he places his hand in her lap. In the final moments of the 'talkie' – perhaps representing the hero and heroine united after their moment of peril, each of the couples settles into a more comfortable position, while the schoolboys exchange a glance of contempt at the necessity for 'love stuff' after all the excitement of the drama. Sally, by contrast completely relaxes against Harry's shoulder – replete and satisfied with the resolution of the drama, as the light from the screen, falling on her face, fades along with the images of the film. The scene ends with the musicians suddenly coming to life to play the National Anthem, as the house lights go up and the audience stand to attention in deference to the evocation of the monarch, a practice standard in British cinemas and theatres of the period.

The examples cited above suggest the range and complexity of audiences' experiences of cinema-going throughout the silent period. Cinemas certainly became larger and more luxurious towards the end of 1920s, and the films which they showed became longer and arguably more complex, but the experience of cinema-going itself was always made up of a heady combination of physical and mental stimulation. The images and stories onscreen were inseparable from the physical 'event' of the trip to the pictures – the decision of whether to travel to a big city centre 'super' or nip to the local 'cosy'; the thrill of a pristine new film print against the frustration of a ropey old end-of-run print full of scratches and missing sections; the live music – varying wildly in quality from cinema to cinema; the comfort of the upholstered seats against the anxiety of picking up fleas; the ubiquitous smell – a mixture of cigarette smoke and sweat, partially masked by the perfumes that many exhibitors released in their auditoria, or by the astringent pong of Jeyes disinfectant fluid which the ushers, pacing up and down the aisles, sometimes sprayed on the audience. The very physicality of the experience is easy to forget when watching old films on modern formats such as DVD or YouTube. A vivid illustration of how different the experience may have been is provided by an advert in the *Kinematograph Weekly* (a magazine aimed at cinema managers in Britain) in 1921. It reprints a news story from the *Daily Sketch*:

> At Stoke Newington, in consequence of the fog, picture palaces had to close, and thousands of persons who had promised themselves an enjoyable evening had to return home. The fog in the interiors of the halls was so thick that the powerful lamps were unable to penetrate from the operator's box to the screen.

Help was at hand however. The advertiser, Castleton-Knight (manager of the Majestic, Clapham) declares that he has beaten the fog. 'I can show a perfect picture through any fog,' he declares to other managers, and 'by courtesy of my Directors I can do the same for you' (Anon. 1921: 39).

Note

1   An American remake of this film, *Uncle Josh at the Moving Pictures* (Thomas Edison, 1902) shows 'Uncle Josh' watching the film from a box

in the theatre. At its climax, he rushes towards the screen in an attempt to remonstrate with the projected figures, and in his passion pulls the screen down, revealing the projectionist behind and destroying the illusion.

2 GERMANY – BEYOND 'EXPRESSIONISM'

At a performance of *Dr Caligari* the other day a shadow shaped like
a tadpole suddenly appeared at one corner of the screen. It swelled
to an immense size, quivered, bulged, and sank back again into
nonentity. For a moment it seemed to embody some monstrous
diseased imagination of the lunatic's brain. For a moment it
seemed as if thought could be conveyed by shape more effectively
than by words. The monstrous quivering tadpole seemed to be fear
itself, and not the statement 'I am afraid'...
> – Virginia Woolf, *The Cinema* (1926: 382)

It is perhaps not surprising that in her quest for a cinematic language that
could offer a 'new symbol for expressing thought', Virginia Woolf should
turn to Germany's most famous and influential film of the period, *The
Cabinet of Dr Caligari*. Its critical and commercial success helped paved the
way for the lifting of a post-war resistance to German cinema in America,
France and Britain, opening up markets that had previously been closed
to German producers. In 1919, with hostilities fresh in the memory, British
and US commentators had argued for a ban on German film imports, not
just because their superior quality presented a commercial threat to home
producers, but also because it was felt that they were likely to encode
'German' attitudes of mind which were inimical to the impeccable morals
of allied audiences. German films, it was assumed, would be 'beastly',

'nasty in their appeal' and likely to rely on themes that were best 'left to the laboratory, the hospital, the eugenicist, and the unmoral highbrow' (Anon. 1919a: 67).

It is ironic then, that the film that swept away this prejudice against German cinema, and which has since become synonymous with that cinema, was celebrated precisely for its unsettlingly macabre qualities, its emphasis on disordered psychology, its allusion to a national 'trauma' in wartime defeat, and its innovations in cinematic language. These qualities marked *The Cabinet of Dr Caligari* out as a serious work of cinematic 'art' (a 'highbrow' film) and established a more general perception of German cinema as one of psychological enquiry and artistic innovation. The striking visual design of the film, in particular – its use of highly stylised sets emphasising distorted perspectives, curious angles and looming shadows – alongside the suggestion that these distortions were an expression of the distorted psychology of its protagonists, led the film to be labelled 'expressionist' in style. The term was borrowed from movements in the visual arts and in theatre design which had been popular around 1910 but which had more or less died out by 1920 (see Roberts 2008: 15). Applied to cinema 'German expressionism' took on a new meaning, and indeed was cultivated by producers as a sort of brand identity – a way of selling German films internationally as a particular kind of artistic product (see Elsaesser 2000: 26). The label still dominates most accounts of that cinema today.

Beyond 'Expressionism'

German cinema of the 1920s was marked by a remarkable degree of technical innovation and originality – elements that enhanced its international reputation as a quality art cinema. Nevertheless, such films did not account for the whole, or even the majority, of Germany's output in the period. As Joseph Garncarz notes, the German industry above all produced popular commercial entertainment films, built around genres and stars; its output was prodigious, accounting for almost half of the total number of films produced within the whole of Europe between 1920 and 1929 (2003: 389). The most popular genres revolved around themes very different from those associated with expressionism. War films, mountain films, operettas and military comedies are listed by Garncarz as the key genres which found favour with German audiences, and many of these (particularly the operettas and comedies) were adapted from the already existing popular traditions of the theatre. Many of these films no longer survive, and most are not readily available to view. The general reader, for instance, would struggle to get hold of one of the many light comedies, drawing on plots and settings from the world of operetta, that were produced by Frederich Zelnik, despite their popularity with audiences during the 1920s. The comedies and history dramas of Ernst Lubitsch and the series of 'mountain' films starring Leni Riefenstahl are more readily accessible, perhaps thanks to the very different later careers of their makers, and these will be discussed here.

The internationally famous 'expressionist' films present a different problem. While most people would cite *The Cabinet of Dr Caligari*, *Nosferatu* (F. W. Murnau, 1922) and perhaps *Metropolis* (Fritz Lang, 1927) as the most famous examples, opinion remains divided as to how far they constitute a consistent aesthetic 'school' of filmmaking and how widely the term can be applied beyond those well known titles. For Ian Roberts, 'expressionism' refers primarily to the use of light and shadow to create a chiaroscuro effect, portraying 'artificial worlds' and dreamscapes of 'such visual abundance that they sit on the border between reality and fantasy, creating oneiric visions of great richness' (2008: 5). He draws on Kristin Thompson's observation that such films strive for a consistent compositional vision, binding together the various elements of *mise-en-scène* – lighting, costume, performance and setting. The dominant filmmaking practice in Germany was to shoot entirely in the studio, where control could be exerted over every element of the production. This, coupled with an industrial structure which encouraged close, long-term collaborations between particular directors and their favoured lighting designers, set designers, cameramen and scriptwriters, ensured an auteurist cinema well suited to the realisation of these 'expressionist' visions. For Roberts these visual and industrial factors mean that the 'expressionist' label can be extended un-problematically to include films from very late in the period, such as *Asphalt* (Joe May, 1929), a film with a visual style and thematic concerns quite different to those of the uncanny fantasies of the early 1920s.

Others advocate a much narrower use of the term. While an emphasis on the 'world of light and shadow' is evident across many of the celebrated films of the period, there seems to be quite a radical aesthetic difference between the static shadows quite literally painted onto the flat sets of *The Cabinet of Dr Caligari* and those created in light for the climactic scene of *Nosferatu*, let alone the extraordinary three-dimensional optical illusions created for *Metropolis*, or the dynamic camera movements of *The Last Laugh* (F. W. Murnau, 1924). Scholars such as Barry Salt and Sabine Hake have argued for a much stricter definition of 'expressionism'. As Hake states, 'Whilst expressionist elements can be found in a number of genres and oeuvres, only a few films aimed at a radical transformation of the visible world, a projection of psychological states into highly constructed filmic spaces (2002: 29). She cites only seven films, all made before 1925, including *The Golem: How He Came Into the World* (Paul Wegener, 1920), *Warning Shadows* (Arthur Robinson, 1923), *The Hands of Orlac* (Robert Weine, 1924) and *Waxworks* (Paul Leni, 1924). Despite the high level of 'brand recognition' for 'German expressionism', then, most scholars today prefer the term 'Weimar cinema', an aesthetically neutral term which refers to the political regime that prevailed in Germany between the abdication of the Kaiser in 1919 through to Hitler's assumption of power in 1933.

The Weimar Republic was born out of extreme political and social unrest. The National Assembly that declared it had relocated to the small historic city of Weimar to avoid the heavy street fighting that had been continuing in Berlin and other large industrial centres since the collapse of the previous regime in the autumn of 1918, and the political chaos following Germany's defeat in the First World War. The Republic retained only a fragile authority throughout its early years, which were marked in particular by economic instability up to 1924. A combination of war debts, reparations payments demanded by the Versailles treaty, and the policy of overprinting paper money in an attempt to buy foreign currency with which to pay these debts, led to a period of rapid devaluation of the German currency and consequent hyperinflation. Perhaps counter-intuitively, this period of economic instability proved advantageous for German film producers. It made Germany an unattractive export market for Hollywood producers, who were aggressively expanding into other European territories, such as Britain, during this period. The rapid devaluation of the German mark meant that profits made by American films at the German box office would have melted away by the time they got back to California, and consequently German producers enjoyed an almost free reign in their home market. High unemployment also kept labour and production costs low. Finally, those producers with the necessary resources had an incentive to invest in prestige films aimed at foreign markets, because if such films were successful abroad (as early hits such as *The Cabinet of Dr Caligari* and Lubitch's 1919 historical epic *Madame DuBarry*, a.k.a. *Passion*, were) then the profits came in the form of foreign currencies, which held their value. Thus a policy that emphasised prestige productions, showcasing a version of German cinema that appealed to international audiences (and often drew on 'expressionist' techniques), was devised during the period of hyperinflation. German producers continued to pursue it throughout the remainder of the decade. It perhaps explains the emphasis on auteur-dominated production units noted by Roberts. After 1924, the currency was revalued and the economic position stabilised, partly as a result of extensive loans from America. The increased economic stability was reflected in the renewed interest of Hollywood producers in the German market, as they invested heavily in the German film industry in exchange for the right to distribute some of their own products across German territories. Scholars also mark the stabilisation of 1924 as the beginning of a shift towards new styles and themes. Styles such as 'New Objectivity', the 'Kammerspielfilm' and the 'Street' films offered the opportunity to explore more contemporary themes, reflecting on modernity, on the lives of ordinary people, on the new consumer culture and on questions of gender and sexuality which accompanied the economic stability of the latter half of the decade. The main case study in this chapter will look at some of the ways in which these themes play out in the late 1920s film *Asphalt*. Perhaps then, the term 'Weimar cinema' is not so neutral after all, for it encourages an understanding of the films partly as an index of the political and social changes taking place in Germany both before and after 1924.

The most influential writer on German cinema of the 1920s is Siegfried Kracauer. Loosely connected with the Frankfurt School of social theorists (he was a close friend of Theodor Adorno), Kracauer worked as a journalist and critic in Berlin throughout the 1920s, and it was here that he developed his approach to popular cinema as a mass communication phenomenon. Like Adorno and other broadly socialist commentators of the period, he approached mass culture from a very ambivalent perspective, considering it to be a product of capitalist endeavour and therefore unlikely to offer anything but a support for the capitalist status quo. He considered film, in particular, less as an art from, or as an industrial product, but rather as a sort of psychological and ideological repository of German society. 'Films are the mirror of the prevailing society', he declared in 1927, but he later refined this position to suggest a more symbiotic relationship between films and their audiences (1995: 291). Films, he argued the following year, not only created, but *were created by* the tastes and aspirations of their audiences. Producers were not 'alone responsible for their commodity. In order to survive they must try to satisfy the needs of the consumers... The critique of current film production is thus by no means directed exclusively against the industry, but focuses just as much on the public sphere which allows it to flourish. Lie together, die together...' (1995: 307). As is evident in his tone, Kracauer was not particularly sympathetic to the tastes of the mass audience, or of the products designed to serve it. His was a social critique which found in cinema evidence for a deep-seated and firmly held conservatism at all levels of German society. He characterised the cinema audience, in particularly classist and gendered terms, as 'little shopgirls', or (after 1924) as the 'low-level white-collar workers, whose number has increased not only in absolute but also in relative terms since the rationalisation of our economy' (ibid.). Nevertheless, the social complacency that he claimed to see embodied in the cinema reached all levels of society. It wasn't that the films themselves were realistic – rather it was that they revealed an underlying reality in the way that people thought:

> There is no kitsch one could invent that life itself could not outdo. Servant girls do not imitate professional love-letter writers; rather, the opposite is true – the latter model their letters on those of servant girls... Sensational film hits and life usually correspond to each other because the Little Miss Typists model themselves after the examples they see on the screen... Stupid and unreal film fantasies are the *daydreams of society*, in which its actual reality comes to the fore and its otherwise repressed wishes take on form. (1995: 292)

It would be some years before Kracauer was able to develop these ideas about the relationship between film and society into a complete history of Weimar cinema. When he did so, from exile in America between 1941 and 1943, events in his homeland during the intervening period suggested a compelling narrative trajectory to his ideas. The book he published was provocatively entitled *From Caligari to Hitler: A Psychological History of the German Film* (1947). The startling claim which the title seemed to make – that it was possible to trace through a study of the films of the Weimar period the social and cultural conditions, but more importantly, the national psychological disposition which allowed (or perhaps even helped bring about) the rise of Hitler – was confirmed in the very first line of the book's preface. Every account of Weimar cinema that has since been published has had to find a way of responding to this startling thesis. Critics have pointed to the highly selective way in which Kracauer chose certain films – films which seemed to confirm his thesis – for extended discussion, while ignoring or skimming over others. They have criticised the teleological assumption behind the thesis (the idea that films can somehow predict the future) and have emphasised instead the ways in which the films sought to process the immediate past – particularly the trauma of national defeat and humiliation in 1918. They have suggested alternative models of spectatorship, ones which offer the 'little shopgirls' and the 'low-level white-collar workers' more agency to create their own meanings from their viewing than perhaps Kracauer had allowed, and they have pointed to the sometimes quite one-sided readings he offers of films which are ambiguous enough to invite a variety of competing interpretations. Nevertheless, while his analysis may be flawed in all of these ways, Kracauer's model of cinema as both moulded by and responding to the social, political and ideological changes of the society that produces it, is still the basis for most accounts of popular film today.

Caligari, Oysters and Dolls

The screening of *The Cabinet of Dr Caligari* to which Virginia Woolf refers in the opening quote was most likely the one hosted by the London Film Society on 14 March 1926. Woolf was a member of the Society, which had been founded the previous year. It was devoted to repertory screenings and revivals of important films that had demonstrated 'improvements in technique', and which were therefore worthy of serious study. That *The Cabinet of Dr Caligari* (already six years old at that point) was chosen for revival, indicates its status within intellectual film circles. Woolf's interest in the film was that it seemed to hold out the possibility that cinema might develop into a completely new language, one that could convey psychological states in purely abstract visual terms – something indisputably *cinematic*. She contrasted it against American cinema, which she found tediously literal in its attempts to symbolise emotion – 'A kiss is love,' she complained, 'a broken cup is jealousy. A grin is happiness. Death is a hearse.' Her experience in the screening suggested the possibility of a new symbolic system, where anger might be conveyed, not by 'red faces and clenched fists' but by 'a black line wiggling on a white sheet'. Woolf's encounter with *The Cabinet of Dr Caligari* is often cited, but most writers omit to mention that the film turned out not to be abstract enough for her. She dismisses the thrilling effect of the 'monstrous quivering tadpole' in her next sentence, admitting that 'in fact, the shadow was accidental and the effect unintentional' (1926: 382). Perhaps there was just a bit of fluff caught in the projector?

Despite Woolf's disappointment, the reputation of *The Cabinet of Dr Caligari* rests precisely on its expressive qualities – on its rejection of photographic realism, and its emphasis on conveying, in visual terms, the disordered psychology of its characters (see Robinson 1997: 7). Most famously, this is achieved through its distorted sets, and through its complex flashback structure, a series of stories told by different narrators, none of whom, as we discover, can be trusted. Looking back ten years from 1930, Paul Rotha remembered the film's appearance as 'like a drop of wine in an ocean of salt water' (1967: 93). It was, he recalled 'once and for all, the first attempt at the expression of a creative mind in the new medium of cinematography' – the film which finally demonstrated

> that a film, instead of being realistic, might be a possible reality, both imaginative and creative; that a film could be effective dramatically when not photographic; and finally, of the greatest possible importance, that the mind of the audience was brought into play psychologically. (1967: 96)

The film opens with two men sitting on a bench in a wintery garden. They are in mid-conversation, and although the décor and surroundings seem naturalistic enough, there is something slightly off-key about their behaviour and expressions. They stare forwards, rather than looking at one another. When they speak, the close-ups showing them talking are irised, isolating them from their surroundings and each other. A woman appears, moving through the space in what seems like a trance. She passes close to the men, who stare at her intently, although she shows no sign of seeing or recognising them. 'That is my fiancée', declares Francis (Friedrich Feher) excitedly to his companion in an inter-title. 'What she and I have experienced is even stranger than what you have lived through... Let me tell you about it.' From the very start, then, *The Cabinet of Dr Caligari* is established as a story told by one man to another, and a story whose primary characteristic is its 'strangeness'. The editing employed to make the transition from this framing scene to the 'flashback' story also emphasises the idea that we are seeing the story through Francis's eyes. A shot of his fiancée moving further off is followed by an answering close-up of Francis, apparently still gazing at her as he speaks to his companion. Holding his gaze, he makes a gesture with his hand as though to conjure the vision that follows in the next shot – a vision of 'the little town where I was born'. The image is unlike any of the others seen so far – it is a flat painting, like a stylised theatrical backdrop or a picture from a child's book, representing a little medieval town clustered higgledy-piggledy on a hilltop. It vanishes, to be replaced by another, wider shot of the same image, now actually functioning as a backdrop in what could be a theatre set. In front of it are stylised representations of the tents and covered stalls announced in an inter-title as 'The annual fair in Holstenwall'. Unlike the previous inter-titles, this one is not in quotation marks – it's not identified as a quotation of Francis's speech, but rather as an announcement of location by the film itself. Nevertheless, the film is still not ready to relinquish Francis's point of view. It cuts back to him, gazing intently into the camera, as though seeing the vision he has conjured. Suddenly his expression changes to one of fear and he shrinks back exclaiming, 'That's him!' In the little stylised world of Holstenwall a figure emerges from the clutter of tents. It is Dr Caligari (Werner Krauss) in the top hat, cape, gloves, cane and high collar of a nineteenth-century businessman. He pugnaciously approaches the camera, gazing into the lens as an iris obscures the background, concentrating our attention on his face. The shot is matched by the return gaze of Francis, reeling with fear at the presence of Caligari in his vision.

From this point onwards, the stylised world of Holstenwall takes over as we learn Francis's story. He and his friend Alan (Hans von Twardowski) are rivals for the love of Jane (Lil Dagover). Excitedly they prepare to visit the fairground. Meanwhile Caligari visits the town hall in order to obtain a permit to exhibit his attraction at the fair – a somnambulist. The town clerk is high handed and treats him disrespectfully, leaving Caligari fuming. That night the clerk is murdered in his bed. Francis and Alan see Caligari's show. In a coffin-like box he displays Cesare (Conrad Veidt), a 23-year-old somnambulist who spends 'day and night without interruption' in a death-like sleep, but 'knows every secret … knows the past and sees the future'. He only wakes at Caligari's command to demonstrate these amazing powers of prediction by answering questions from his audience. Alan pushes forward and asks the question that, as Anton Kaes has noted, must have been in the mind of every young man in the years of war immediately before the film's production: 'How long do I have to live?' (2009: 52). The answer delivered by Cesare appalls him: 'Until dawn tomorrow.' Returning home, they see a notice detailing the clerk's murder and their sense of foreboding increases. Sure enough, in the night Alan too is murdered in his bed.

The Cabinet of Doctor Caligari is often cited in discussions about the origins of the expressionist use of shadows to create a mood of foreboding, breaking up the image on the screen to make it mysterious, uncanny or hyper-real. In fact, despite the abundance of all of these qualities in the film, the scene of Alan's murder is the only one that uses actual shadows created by lighting to convey such effects. As Alan lies sleeping, the mon-

Fig. 3: *The Cabinet of Dr. Caligari* (1919); stylised design – a 'splash of light' from the window is painted onto the set, while the murderer is shown in a shadow silhouette.

strous silhouette of a head looms in shadow on the wall above him. He wakes and looking off-screen to the source of the shadow, screams.

There is a close-up of him screaming, and then a closer version of the first shot, which shows only the wall above the bed, where in silhouette we see him struggling as his attacker draws a knife. The scene is striking not only for its innovative use of such shadows, but also because in other scenes of the film, shadows are not created in light, but *physically painted* onto the floors and walls of the sets. In the sets of interiors (in Alan's living room and in the town clerk's bedroom and on the staircase leading up to the police station, for instance), distorted window shapes are painted on the walls and floors to convey either the windows themselves, or the window-shaped splashes of light cast onto interior walls at odd angles by streetlights. Indeed, the very wall on which we witness the shadow of Alan's murder includes such an effect (in this instance created with shapes of pale fabric glued to the walls), drawing attention to the unreality of both strategies of representation. A similar effect is created in the preceding scene of the town square just before the friends discover the notice of the clerk's murder. The square consists of a series of painted flats and stylised street furniture. A distorted water pump is in the background, and in the foreground is a street lamp attached to the gable of a building, which seems to be falling into the square. The lamp is unlit, until a lamplighter crosses the set and lights it – but even before it has been lit, an irregular white star shape is visible, painted on the ground below it to represent the light it casts.

After Alan's murder, Francis is convinced that Caligari is using his power over Cesare to hypnotise him into committing the horrible deeds. Jane confirms these suspicions after Cesare attempts to kidnap her, and Francis pursues the fleeing Caligari who eventually disappears behind the walls of an insane asylum. When Francis enquires after the 'patient' he is introduced to the Director of the asylum instead, and is appalled to discover that the Director is Caligari himself. Raving, he rushes away. Later while the Director is asleep, some of the staff assist Francis to investigate. The Director's special area of study is somnambulism, they discover, and among his papers is an account of a 'Dr Caligari' who in 1703 toured the fairgrounds with a 'somnambulist' called Cesare, and in whose wake a series of terrible murders were committed. This information is conveyed through a series of inter-titles showing the printed account intercut with shots of the four men avidly reading it. Next, they find the Director's diary, and the account they read here is conveyed in the inter-titles (now hand-written), but also enacted by the film, thus introducing a second flashback, and a second 'narrator' – the Director/Caligari himself. This ambiguity is heightened by a series of cutaway shots, which show the Director asleep in his bed. Is what we see a faithful representation of the diary's record, or is it a dream that the Director/Caligari is having? How far is its veracity to be trusted, given that it is still also a visualisation of the story being told in the conversation between the two men on the bench in the opening scene? The diary entries speak of the excitement the Director feels on the admission to the asylum of a somnambulist. At last he can fulfill his ambition of reproducing the psychiatric experiments of his hero, the Caligari of 1703. 'Now I shall learn if it's true that a somnambulist can be compelled to perform acts which, in a waking state, would be abhorrent to him ... whether, in fact, he can be driven against his will to commit a murder.'

Whether, in fact, he can be driven against his will to commit murder. This was, perhaps, a question that the generation of 1914–18 was uniquely in a position to answer. 'No somnambulism needed,' they might have replied, 'only propaganda, conscription and the rule of law.' Although, as Kaes points out, it is worth noting that we've already seen Cesare resist the Director's command, when he failed to murder Jane (2009: 67). The images show us the Director 'in the grip of an obsession', his fists clenched tight as he pours over the writings of his hero, he clutches the book close to him and gestures upwards to the ceiling. 'I must know everything – I must penetrate the heart of his secret – I must *become Caligari*', he declares in an inter-title. And here the inter-titles and the image merge as he rushes out into the night, raving and gesticulating. The words 'Du musst Caligari werden' literally appear in the sky, and he staggers towards them. In the branches of a tree they appear, and again above his head. The name 'Caligari' repeats all about him as he retreats, raving from the scene. Again, one asks, who is the author of this scene? Is it the Director's feverish dream? Is this mania recorded in his diary (the inter-titles are no longer hand-written but in the stylised script that has been used throughout the film)? Is it an embellishment of Francis's as he recounts his story to his companion in the garden? When later the Director/Caligari is confronted with his duel identity, and presented with the unconscious body of Cesare, he appears to break down again, and is carted off in a straightjacket. The film finally cuts back from the stylised world to Francis and his companion on the bench in the garden, where Francis is concluding his story: 'and from that day on, the madman has never left his cell.' But who is the madman? As they rise and walk through the garden, it becomes evident that it *is* the garden of the asylum, and the two men are inmates. Cesare and Jane are there too. And when the Director appears – not raving this time, but apparently quite sane – it is the Director/Caligari himself. Francis has a breakdown at the sight of him, attacking him and declaring 'You all think I'm insane! It isn't true, it's the Director who's insane!... He is Caligari... Caligari... Caligari!' In a mirror of the preceding scene, Francis is now carried off in a straightjacket to a cell. He is attended by the Director, who declares that finally he understands Francis's delusion and as a result will be able to cure him.

The Cabinet of Dr Caligari, then, is revealed to be a tale told by a madman. The crazy distortions, abstractions and gestures of the settings might be explained as projections of Francis's own delusional worldview. This was an interpretation that infuriated Kracauer. Recounting what we now understand to be a misleading account of the film's production, he suggested that the framing scenes at the beginning and end of the film, showing Francis recounting the story and then revealing him to be an inmate of the asylum, were added by the director and producer against the will of the film's writers (see Robinson 1997: 8–24). Kracauer argued that this addition allowed a 'rational explanation' for the stylised settings, which was a betrayal of the film's original radicalism. If the producers had left it as the writers had intended,

> these 'drawings brought to life' would have told it perfectly. As expressionist abstractions they were animated by the same revolutionary spirit that impelled the two scriptwriters who accuse authority – the kind of authority revered in Germany – of inhuman excess. However, Wiene's version disavowed this revolutionary meaning of expressionist staging, or, at least, put it, like the original story itself, in brackets. (1947: 70)

As a result, he claimed, instead of 'exposing the madness inherent in authority', the film 'glorified authority and convicted its antagonist of madness. A revolutionary film was thus turned into a conformist one' (1947: 60). Few viewers today would agree with this rather cut-and-dried interpretation. For one thing, as Kracauer himself notes, the final sequence still employs the same stylised settings as the earlier scenes, even after Francis's narrative has ended and his apparent insanity revealed. When he is thrown into a cell, it is one composed of curious diagonals, sharp angles and painted shadows. In fact, it is the very same cell that the Director was previously thrown into in Francis's 'deluded' version of the story. The film's profound suspicion over the legitimacy of authority is evident throughout – not only in the portrayal of Caligari as a brutal monster, controlling both Cesare and, through the terror he creates, the whole town – but also in its representation of lesser authority figures. The arrogant town clerk and the policemen, for instance, are all shown perched on ludicrously tall stools, towering over the people who petition them. Certainly the final sequence leaves plenty of doubt about whether 'the Director' is actually sane or whether he has simply managed to trump reason, persuading or terrorising those around him into accepting his authority, even though he has in fact *become Caligari*.

Following Kracauer, *The Cabinet of Dr Caligari* has frequently been read as responding metaphorically to the trauma of 1918 and a loss of faith with Germany's wartime leaders, but also with the idea of leadership itself. The themes articulated within the film – the malevolence of authority, the fragility of male identity, the fear of a descent into madness, the trauma of personal humiliation and loss of agency – have been traced through a whole range of German films made during the early 1920s. To cite some famous examples, in *The Golem* a medieval rabbi fashions a monstrous Golem out of clay and brings him to life using a sacred text placed in the Golem's chest. Initially the monster gains the Jews' patronage from the local Emperor, but later the rabbi loses control of him and he rampages through the city intent on destruction. In *Nosferatu*, a young couple come under the spell of a vampire, who terrorises their town, spreading death and discord. Only by the sacrifice of the hero's wife can the vampire be vanquished and order restored. In *The Hands of Orlac*, a concert pianist loses his hands in a terrible train crash. A brilliant surgeon transplants the hands of a recently executed murderer onto him, but when his father is killed in mysterious circumstance, he begins to believe his new hands have retained their old habits. In *The Last Laugh*, a hotel porter suffers a loss of pride when he is demoted to the position of a washroom attendant on account of his advancing years. He attempts to hide this humiliating change of status from his family and his community, but when they discover his shame, they reject him. Each of these films is celebrated, not only for its thematic resonance, but also for the technical skill with which it builds on the expressive use of design, lighting, performance style and narrative ambiguity evident in *The Cabinet of Dr Caligari*.

Nevertheless, this is not the whole story. A useful corrective might be found in the example of the comedies being made by Ernst Lubitsch around the same time as *The Cabinet of Dr Caligari*. In films like *The Doll* and *The Oyster Princess* (both 1919) one searches in vain for the kinds of macabre themes mentioned above, or even for evidence of the 'trauma' of Germany's wartime defeat. The filmmakers were certainly not insulated from the events of the November revolution – one account suggests that the sounds of street fighting even penetrated the screening rooms of the Berlin studios where they worked (see Fischer 2009). Nevertheless, the films themselves show no trace of that history. Sabina Hake suggests that they instead 'present a challenge to widespread notions about early German cinema, and expressionist film in particular', and can be seen as 'part of an equally powerful, but suppressed tradition', which used visual design, overt performance styles and cinematic self-reflexivity to emphasise not psychological trauma, but play, spectacle and pleasure. Most importantly, such films were built around independent, high-spirited female stars (in this case Ossi Oswalda), who provided new opportunities for female identification, and the representation of female desire. As Hake states, 'By offering cheerful solutions to the problem of sexual difference, the Lubitsch comedies ... convey a rare sense of joyful eroticism (1992: 82).

The playfulness and self-reflexivity of *The Doll* are triumphantly established from the very beginning. The first inter-title announces it as 'four amusing acts from a toy box' and the introductory scene literalises that description. Lubitsch, the director, is shown opening an enormous toy box, out of which he retrieves each of the elements of the opening scene, and puts them together like a child's theatre. First a raked floor depicting a grassy meadow with a winding path is laid out, then a little house and some trees are affixed to this ground. Some foreground treetrunks are added, emphasising the forced perspective of the design, then a little bench and a backdrop to frame the scene. There is a cut to a closer view of the 'set'

Fig. 4: *The Doll* (1919); stylised design – the director 'builds' the set from the contents of a toy box.

as Lubitsch adds two little doll figures, and then places them inside the house, popping them in through a hinged roof. A final cut transforms the scene from the model to a life-size film set, although still with the stylised design of the toy set. Two real-life actors emerge from the little house and the story begins.

Like the opening sequence of *The Cabinet of Dr Caligari*, this scene draws attention to the constructed-ness of the story world in which the film will take place. The scenic design is self-consciously stylised – not, in this instance, to convey expressionistically the distortions of a sick mind, or to highlight the unreliability of the storyteller (although, significantly, attention *is* drawn to the presence of Lubitsch as the storyteller – an acknowledgement rarely afforded the director in this period). Rather, the designs of *The Doll* seem to emphasise the film's mythic, fairy tale qualities, reminding the audience at all times of its generic status as a comedy – a space for pleasure and escape. The sun and moon appear in the story, smiling and frowning on the events they observe, as in a child's book. At one point the hero and heroine ride in a carriage drawn by pantomime horses who sit back like dogs when their journey is over and remonstrate with the coachman about their statutory period of rest. Even so, as in all comedies, some fundamental ideas about the relationship between gender, money and power are being worked through. The figures in the doll's house are Lancelot and his maid. They are summoned by his uncle, the Baron von Chanterelle, who orders Lancelot to take a wife, in order that he might continue the Baron's dynastic line. The idea of marrying appals Lancelot, but word has already got around the town and he is chased through the market square by a hoard of young maidens, keen to get their hands on him and the generous financial settlement the Baron has announced on anyone who will take him on. This chase again is filmed in a highly stylised manner – Lancelot enters the scene on the left, runs down a flight of stairs, around the fountain, and off to the right, and all of his pursuers follow this exact route, ignoring the obvious advantage they would gain by omitting the fountain. The shot is held until all the pursuers have vanished out of the frame, and then Lancelot appears again from the back of the set to be pursued on another tortuous route, as if in a pantomime. Eventually he takes refuge in a monastery, where the monks, on hearing of his plight and spying an opportunity to bag some of the financial settlement for themselves, recommend a doll-maker who can make life-like dolls who can walk, dance and sing on command. This way, they suggest, he will be able to satisfy his uncle, collect the money, and yet remain free of the pernicious influence of a real-life wife. The doll-maker's catalogue is quite explicit about the tenor of his customers, advertising his dolls as for the use of 'bachelors, widowers and misogynists'! When Lancelot visits the showroom, he finds the dolls on display rather too sexually brazen for his taste. The only one that appeals to him is modelled on the doll-maker's own daughter Ossi (Ossi Oswalda). Little does he know that this doll is in fact Ossi herself who has had to make a last-minute substitution after the doll modelled on her was broken. The rest of the film turns on Ossi's increasingly desperate attempts to maintain the illusion that she *is* a doll throughout their extravagant wedding, despite growing increasingly hungry, thirsty and tired. Eventually, having fooled the whole court, they return to the monastery and she manages to overpower the monks (who are intent on locking her up in the junk cupboard) and return to Lancelot to reveal her true identity and gain his hand (and the cash) for real.

   The Doll has attracted nothing like the critical attention afforded *The Cabinet of Dr Caligari*, despite the fact that both films share an emphasis on stylisation and the foregrounding of narrator figures. As Hake suggests, there are other similarities – both films 'focus on the theme of creation and mastery' in the figures of Caligari and the doll-maker (1992: 94). While anxieties over male agency are highlighted in *The Cabinet of Dr Caligari* through metaphors of control, sleepwalking, dream-like states and delusions, in *The Doll* male figures are generally ridiculed – hopelessly inadequate, venal or simply foolish. Yet the film's use of masquerade as a trope, Hake argues, is key to its representation of femininity:

> By pretending to be a more perfect woman (i.e. a doll), the woman is able to enjoy the privileges denied her in a male dominated society... *The Doll* tells the refreshing tale of a woman who, by being turned into an object of male desire, turns against that order. (1992: 98, 102)

The Oyster Princess also centres on a marriage arranged as a contract but manipulated and triumphantly moulded into a satisfactory love-match by its lively and appealing heroine, again played by Ossi Oswalda. Here she plays the imperious daughter of an American oyster millionaire who demands a groom of suitable noble status – a prince, in fact – no matter whether or not he is impoverished. The prince's hapless footman pays Ossi and her father a visit to ascertain their suitability, and through a series of misunderstandings, gets scooped up as the groom in a variety of eye-poppingly extravagant nuptial celebrations. Only later, when Ossi has by chance met and fallen in love with the (rather inadequate and drunken) real prince, is the mistake discovered and rectified. The comedy of *The Oyster Princess* is predicated on ludicrous excess – particularly that of the American father and daughter in their wealth and consumption. The wedding breakfast is served by veritable armies of footmen, moving forward in serried ranks to serve lobsters and pour champagne – a sort of parody of Ford's production line. The famous sequence showing a 'foxtrot epidemic' breaking out among the wedding guests shows an extravagant band featuring percussion provided by three bass drummers, a hacksaw player, a pistol shot and even a fat-cheeked man being 'played' by a bandmate who slaps his jowls in order to provide syncopation. Guests fill the giant ballroom, observed by phalanxes of servants stationed on a balcony, and even the staff in the kitchen – the waiters with their trouser legs rolled up to the knees – dance around the tables holding trays aloft. Here is a celebration, but also a critique, of the excessive abundance of American commodity culture. The film is a sort of wish fulfillment fantasy, which is perhaps not as unrelated to the problems Germany faced in 1919 as it at first appears. As well as these comedies, Lubitsch specialised in lavish costume dramas, also showcasing female stars in strong central roles, for instance Pola Negri in *Madam Dubarry*, and Henny Porten in *Anna Boleyn*.[1] It was as a result of the success of these films in America that Lubitsch was able to find work there, initially directing for Mary Pickford. He moved to Hollywood permanently from 1922 onwards.

UFA and the later 1920s

The Cabinet of Dr Caligari was made by a company called Decla-Bioscope. *The Doll* and *The Oyster Princess* carried the logo 'Union' indicating that they were made by the Projektions-AG Union (PAGU) company. It wasn't long before both of these film companies were absorbed into perhaps the most famous and certainly the most dominant film-producing company in Germany during this period, the Universum-Film AG, or 'Ufa'.[2] Ufa had been founded in 1917 as part of a government and military initiative to produce high-quality film propaganda – an area in which the military felt Germany was falling behind its enemies. After the war it returned to private hands and concentrated on producing films for entertainment, but it also operated in a wide range of film-related industries. Joseph Garncarz points out the contrast between the German film industry and that of Hollywood; while in Hollywood a small handful of big vertically integrated companies emerged to operate a monopoly on production and exhibition, in Germany a much greater number of small independent production companies existed. He offers the example of 1926 when '81 German companies produced 185 feature-length films and 42 of these companies produced only a single film' (2003: 390). Only Ufa and Emelka were of any size, and even these produced few films by Hollywood standards (twelve and nine respectively in 1926). Nevertheless, they were fully integrated in a way that the other companies weren't, owning production and distribution facilities, and chains of theatres. Ufa in particular diversified into all kinds of film-related businesses, including the publication of tie-in novels and fan magazines. Ufa's dominance of the industry was symbolised by its extraordinarily opulent first-run houses in major cities, particularly its flagship, the 'Ufa Palast Am Zoo', which opened in Berlin in 1919 and remodelled in 1925 according to the latest fashions in American cinemas. Kracauer described it as an 'optical fairyland', a place where audiences could partake in the 'cult of distraction', and he compared film-goers in such palaces to 'communities of worshippers' (1995: 232).

The American influence was not accidental. While to a certain extent producers had been protected from foreign competition during the hyper-inflation years before 1924, increasingly in the latter part of the decade, US companies in particular began to take an interest in Germany as a film market. In contrast to Britain, though (where US films accounted for the vast majority of films shown in local cinemas), Hollywood films, while successful in Germany, never dominated the market. A 1925 law in fact prevented this by restricting foreign imports to 50% and offered import licences to distributors only in proportion to the number of domestic films that they handled. Ufa's most distinctive period came under the direction of Erich Pommer, who came to the company from Decla-Bioscope and oversaw all productions from 1923 to his resignation in 1926. Under Pommer, a range of extremely talented and acclaimed directors worked on films that are still revered today. Pommer's system allowed directors absolute control over their productions and their budgets. While Ufa was flush after the profitable hyper-inflation period, this led to some extraordinary technical innovations, as perfectionist directors drove their collaborators to achieve the effects they desired. For Murnau's *The Last Laugh*, the cameraman Karl Freund developed the 'unchained camera', a technique that freed the camera from its tripod, enabling it to move freely through the complex lifts, corridors and revolving doors of the grand hotel where the film's protagonist works, and even to fly through the air, riding on the sound of a blast from a bass trumpet. For Lang's *Metropolis*, Eugen Schüfftan developed the Shüfftan process, which enabled actors to move in what appeared to be enormous architectural settings, but which were in fact painted mattes created with glass and mirrors. But as the decade continued, such extravagant super-productions, or *Großfilme*, became increasingly unprofitable, and Ufa had to turn elsewhere for an injection of capital. In late 1925, they received extensive loans from Paramount and MGM in exchange for exclusive access to 75% of their first-run cinemas for those companies' Hollywood films, in a deal that became known as the 'Parufamet agreement'. The agreement was viewed as an alarming deve-lopment at the time, and scholars still debate its merits today. Garncarz suggests that it only exacerbated Ufa's financial troubles, because almost all of the American films distributed lost money at the box office, with most losing as much as 10,000 marks each (2003: 397). Thomas J. Saunders paints an even more depressing picture of the terms of the agreement, although he does acknowledge that the policy of producing *Großfilme* for exporting to the American market was already failing before the agreement had been put in place (1994: 69–83). Certainly the eye-watering budget of a film such as *Metropolis* meant that no matter how successful it might have been at the box office, it could never have turned a profit. In 1927 the company was taken over again, this time by the right-wing press baron Alfred Hugenberg. Pommer, who had resigned and gone to America as a result of 'Parufamet', returned as a producer, fitting into a new regime which featured less directorial autonomy, more emphasis on star values and more tightly controlled budgets.

While *Metropolis*, with its excessive running time, extravagant futuristic settings and absolute insistence on urban modernity, is perhaps for most people the paradigm of the *Großfilme*, these characteristics weren't necessarily definitive. The mountain films, or *Bergfilm*, are equality impressive and majestic, although they look back to an idealised relationship with nature, rather than forward to futuristic cities. The most famous example, *The Holy Mountain* (Arnold Franck, 1926) was produced just as Pommer had left Ufa and the company was retrenching. Nevertheless it boasted an impressive budget, the fruits of which are evident on the screen, and was a popular box office success. The film was largely shot on location in the Swiss Alps. The clear vistas of mountain ranges, pristine white snowfields and valleys filled with springtime flowers couldn't be further from the 'expressionist' style, although extensive use is made of chiaroscuro lighting in the interior and night scenes. Figures are also often seen silhouetted against the landscape, in a style reminiscent of the animation films that Lotte Reiniger was making for Ufa at around the same time. The film stars Leni Riefenstahl as Diotima, a dancer who unwittingly causes a jealous rift between two mountaineering friends. Romantic love and sexual desire are represented essentially as a distraction from the high ideals to be found in the beautiful but terrible natural world. The film exhibits a passionate faith in the spiritual purity of physical exertion and the remorseless cruelty of the mountains. 'What does one search for up there?' asks the besotted Diotima. 'One's self' comes the reply. Watching the film today, it is difficult to forget Riefenstahl's later career as Hitler's favoured filmmaker and the director of *The Triumph of the Will* (1933).

Indeed, the director, Franck, also made films throughout the Nazi period, joining the party in 1940. How far the mountain films can be seen to embody ideals that were later incorporated into the ideology of National Socialism remains a topic of debate among scholars. One might, for instance, point to similar themes of rural life lived under the hard, unrelenting forces of nature in French, Norwegian and Swedish films of this period, such as *Faces of Children* (Jacques Feyder, 1925), *The Bridal Party in Hardanger* (Rasmus Breistein, 1926) and *The Strongest* (Alf Sjöberg & Axel Lindblom, 1929) – films which also share a visual affinity with the landscape and particularly with snow, but which tend not to be interrogated ideologically in the way that the *Bergfilm* have been. In any event, the technical perfection of Franck's work is undeniable. It is perhaps most evident in the sequence from *The Holy Mountain* which shows a long-distance ski race – the rhythmic editing and the sheer variety of shots, including some astonishing 'unchained' angles from the skier's point of view, ensure that viewers remain on the edge of their seats throughout.

Asphalt and the Street Film

Although the mountain films offer perhaps an extreme example of the rejection of urban life, even those films that took the contemporary city as their setting and theme were distinctly ambivalent about its benefits. The city as a symbol of modernity, of consumption and of pleasure became increasingly prevalent in the late 1920s – a visible result of the economic recovery after 1924, and the showcase for modern technologies of leisure of which cinema was perhaps the most perfect example. For only a small amount of money anyone could partake in the brave new world of leisure, luxury and spectacle represented by a visit to an *Ufa Palast*, signing themselves up to Kracauer's 'culture of distraction'. 'It cannot be overlooked,' he warned in 1926, 'that there are *four million* people in Berlin. The sheer necessity of their circulation transforms the life of the street into the ineluctable street of life giving rise to configurations that invade even domestic space (1995: 325). This 'life of the street' was the subject of a cycle of films that began with *The Street* (Karl Grune, 1923) and arguably ended with *Asphalt* (1929). The films, with their emphasis on contemporary city life, and particularly on the figure of the sexual or criminal woman, share some elements with the 'New Objectivity' of G. W. Pabst, although Hake suggests that the cycle was able to accommodate a wide range of styles, 'from conventional melodrama with a strong dose of Wilhelmine morality, to sleek city symphonies with a more pragmatic, and occasionally also more cynical, attitude to love and sexuality' (2002: 41).[3]

At the beginning of *The Street*, the life of the street literally invades the domestic space, as Kracauer had suggested. The unnamed protagonist, a middle-aged man who appears to be a 'low-level white-collar worker', is lounging on his sofa while his wife prepares supper in the next room. From the street lamp outside the window a splash of light is cast on the ceiling above his head, restless with shadows of the life of the street. The shadows resolve themselves into a tantalising image in silhouette – a girl is propositioned by a dandy, and they go off together. Drawn by this vision, the man crosses the room to the window. Longingly, he looks out, and the matching image is a complex process shot – a collage of all that he fantasises must be out there. Images of tramlines and automobiles and idling crowds give way gradually to a laughing clown, fireworks, a rollercoaster and swingboat rides in a 'Lunar park', and then to the face of a beautiful girl, the legs of women walking along the pavement, dancing couples and watching men – the pleasures of urban modernity all expressed in a few seconds. The man's wife, curious, looks out of the window too, but her matching point of view shot shows none of these temptations, only the workaday street, busy at rush hour, as seen from a first-floor window. From the start, then, the film represents the ocular temptations of the street as something responding to desires of men, rather than women, and the young street women who are the object of those desires are contrasted against the domestic housewife. They represent excitement, but also danger, and the temptations of vice. The middle-aged protagonist cannot resist them. Without a second glance at his wife or the supper, he takes his hat and rushes out into the street. Perhaps his first encounter should act as a warning – as he ogles a prostitute who is lounging on a street corner, she transforms before his eyes into a skull. He is only momentarily deterred. Later, he investigates the new cultures of consumer display that the city offers – following an illuminated pavement sign and encountering another young woman as he gazes at the automata in a travel agent's window. Unperturbed by his previous encounter, he follows her through the streets. An optician's sign depicting a large pair of eyes lights up as the pair pass beneath it, giving him another brief pang of conscience, but by now he is in too deep. The woman lures him into a con-trap, and later into a much worse predicament.

The Street was shot entirely in a studio, using a massive and complex street set so that light and effects could be carefully controlled, as was common in German films of the period. The same is true of *Asphalt*, which also combines an interest in the consumer cultures of display and the city with the predatory sexuality of the criminal woman. *Asphalt*, though, is perhaps less punitive towards its characters, and offers a more nuanced view of female sexuality. In her account of the film, Barbara Hales cites a depressing litany of neurologists, criminologists and popular journalists from the Weimar period who claimed a scientifically proven connection between 'feeble-minded' women and criminality. She argues that while the actual crime rate in Germany fell during the 1920s, an anxiety over political violence was redirected by social scientists and popular journalism into concern over a sexualised female-criminal 'type', establishing a terrifying 'evil Other' against which the rational male bourgeois self could be contrasted. The spectacle of affluent, independent young women, spending their leisure time in shopping and consumption offered a perfect target. Hales quotes popular journalist Thomas Wehrling who characterised Berlin itself as a 'whore', and castigated men who mingled in the streets with a generation of 'short-skirted, silk-stockinged females', even bourgeois females, who had rejected their duty of childbirth and motherhood and had 'nothing but the merchandising of their physical charms in mind' (1996: 107).

The famous and remarkable opening of *Asphalt* certainly seems to draw on these discourses. After a title sequence where road workers seem to beat the fiery letters of the title from the asphalt of the street itself, the film offers a brief but virtuoso montage of shots showing real streets filled with automobiles, trams and people, shot from a variety of strange angles and cut together like a mini 'city symphony'. The sequence ends on the image of a caged bird, hanging by a window – a presentiment, perhaps, of the film's ending. The bird is in the apartment of an elderly couple. The camera ranges around the room showing details of their respectable world – jars of provisions, a clock, ornaments on the mantelpiece and a policeman's helmet cast off after a long day. The policeman himself is relaxing with a cigar while his wife reads the papers. 'You know, Father,' she reflects contentedly, establishing the timeframe for the narrative, 'all that happens in the world on a single day?!' For their son, also a policeman, the day is just starting. As he leaves, the camera returns to the caged bird and a complex process shot returns us to the street, superimposing the tranquil bird in the centre of the image with a the frantic montage of cars and buses all around it. The bird dissolves into a hand. The son, Albert (Gustav Fröhlich), is directing the traffic. In his impressive uniform, complete with leather gaiters and helmet, ordering the cars to stop and go, he looks the picture of authoritative masculinity. However, standing right in the centre of a busy junction on a tiny circle of raised paving with nothing to protect him from the traffic, which swirls around him, he also looks vulnerable. As though to drive home this point, one motorist, disobeying Albert's stop signal, swerves to avoid the stream of oncoming traffic and her car mounts the curb of his little traffic island, almost running him over. While other motorists complain vigorously in the snarl up, he courteously issues her a ticket. She is a young woman, beautiful and fashionably attired. His weakness has been established. The film's most audacious sequence follows. The camera leaves Albert, swept along by the crowds of people thronging the street. It finds a street lamp, and a dissolve to the lamp now lit indicates an ellipsis of time. It is evening and the street is enlivened by a myriad of illuminated advertising signs and shop windows. The camera floats independently above the crowds in an arc-like movement. It reveals the entrance to a cinema, and then tracks up the street to show a crowd gathered outside the window of a store advertising *Strümpfe* (stockings). In the window a model is seductively demonstrating the underwear. A short sequence among the onlookers demonstrates the danger of the streets. A woman, transfixed by the goods on display, fails to notice three thieves working together in the press of the crowd – one distracts her while another picks her purse from her bag and passes it back to his associate further away.

Continuing its audacious movement in the display of modern street life, the camera floats back towards the cinema. It passes a jewellers on the corner and turns, as though distracted by a glimpse through the windows of a scene unfolding within. A cut takes us to a closer and more conventionally filmed account of the scene. Else (Betty Amann) is inspecting a tray of diamonds displayed by an elderly jeweller. Dressed in the height of fashion, with a fur collar and a brilliant white cloche hat emphasising her enormous, lustrous eyes, Else is devastatingly attractive. Neither she, nor the jeweller, is unaware of this fact, and while she transfixes him with her eyes, he fails to notice that one of the diamonds has fallen to the floor near her foot. As it sparkles on the carpet, she adroitly steals it by touching it with the end of her umbrella, which has been tipped with putty for this purpose. When the loss is discovered and Else is recalled to the shop, watched by the thronging crowds in the street, it is, of course, Albert who must oversee her arrest. Throwing herself on his mercy in the car to the police station, she pleads poverty and misfortune, weeping ostentatiously into a handkerchief. The sign of her duplicity is that when she sees her sob story starting to take effect on him, she slyly pulls out a compact and touches up her make up. Else, it seems, is definitely in the business of 'merchandising her physical charms'. She inveigles Albert back to her rooms where, in an astonishing sequence, she purposefully seduces him. She actually leaps onto him, clinging to his shoulders, her toes scrabbling for a foothold at the top of his boots. Seen through the eyes of the contemporary commentators cited by Hales, this scene might be read as a ringing confirmation of all those warnings about the ferocity, destructiveness and criminality of untrammelled female sexuality. For modern audiences though, and perhaps even for the 'little shopgirls' who first saw the film, Else offers a thrilling example of a modern woman pushing against the rigid gender roles of her day to express her desires openly and directly. She is certainly the most charismatic character in the film and its central focus of interest. And after the seduction it becomes evident she genuinely does love Albert – enough to try and save him from the trouble she is in. Later, when – still under the illusion that she steals from need – he asks her to marry him, she confronts him with the truth about her criminality. She throws her cosmetics, her jewels, her furs, all the trappings of her feminine construction before him. 'Is that need?', she demands. *Asphalt*, like *The Street*, contrasts two different conceptions of femininity, geographically arranged – one traditional, domestic, mothering, *indoors*; the other modern, public, sexual, *of the street*. It also does the same for masculinity in the contrast between Albert and his father, but also in the tensions it places within Albert – between his uniform and his role as public guardian, and his own desire for satisfaction, emotional and sexual fulfillment. By the end of the film it becomes evident that both masculinity and femininity must be recast for the new age.

Notes

1   These films were released in America as *Passion* and *Deception* respectively.
2   PAGU had been part of Ufa since the latter's founding in 1917. Decla was absorbed in 1921.
3   For further discussion of Pabst, see P. Hutchinson (2017) *Pandora's Box*. London: British Film Institute/Palgrave.

3   RUSSIA – 'OF ALL THE ARTS, THE MOST IMPORTANT FOR US IS THE CINEMA'

'If you have a good newsreel, serious and enlightening pictures, it doesn't really matter if you show some worthless film with them of a more or less usual type to attract the public... As you find your feet ... you will have to expand production, and particularly make headway with useful films among the masses in the cities, and still more in the countryside... You must remember always that of all the arts the most important for us is the cinema.'
– V. I. Lenin (to A. V. Lunacharsky, 1922)

Some doubts have been raised about whether Lenin did in fact tell Anatole Lunacharsky, the People's Commissar for the Enlightenment, that 'of all the arts the most important for us is the cinema'. We only have Lunacharsky's retrospective word for it. But as Richard Taylor has pointed out, that hardly matters because the statement so perfectly encapsulates official policy that it has been quoted in almost every account of Soviet cinema since (1988: 36). Certainly the popular perception of Soviet cinema – cemented by reference to classics such as *Battleship Potemkin* (Sergei Eisenstein, 1925) and *Man With a Movie Camera* (Dziga Vertov, 1929) – is that it is *revolutionary* in every sense of the word. On the one hand it is closely associated with the political revolution that occurred in Russia in 1917. Overtly propagandistic – designed to inspire and galvanise audiences to act in the interests of the Bolshevik ideal, much as a poster or a photomontage image might do – it constructs, as David Bordwell puts it, a 'cinematic mythology of the new regime' (2003: 369). On the other hand, it represents a formal revolution – an *avant-garde* intervention into cinematic language and editing practices whose repercussions were felt far beyond Soviet Russia. The principles of this formal revolution, elaborated and written down by practitioners such as Lev Kuleshov, Sergei Eisenstein, Vsevolod Pudovkin and Dziga Vertov, form the foundational texts of modern film theory. Given the monumental reputation of these figures, and the wide international fame of the films they produced, one might be forgiven for thinking that ordinary cinemagoers in 1920s Russia subsisted exclusively on a diet of revolutionary agitprop classics. In fact this is far from the truth. Such films make up only a handful of those shown in Russia at the time, and the evidence suggests that they were never conspicuously successful at the box office (see Youngblood 1992: 18). Surprising as it may seem, audiences were as likely to find German comedies or American society dramas playing at their local cinema, as revolutionary propaganda. Many cinemas, it seems, followed Lenin's advice quoted above, mixing 'serious and enlightening pictures' with 'worthless films ... of a usual type' designed to guarantee an audience and a profit. Indeed the overall film policy from 1924 onwards enshrined this idea, allowing foreign imports of (from a Soviet point of view) dubious ideological worth, explicitly in order to allow the build up of industrial capital to fund the development of a self-sustaining domestic production industry. The popularity of foreign stars such as Harry Piel and Mary Pickford was widely noted and agonised over, but a significant strand of domestic producers also worked on non *avant-garde* films, producing costume dramas, comedies and social problem films – films such as *The Bear's Wedding* (Konstantin Eggert, 1925), *A Kiss from Mary Pickford* (Sergey Komarov, 1927) and *Bed and Sofa* (Abram Room, 1927) – which rejected montage aesthetics in favour of generic narratives, popular stars and conventional editing structures.

This chapter shall consider the economic and industrial context which encouraged this extraordinary mixture of styles, and offer discussions of examples of each of the three major categories of films circulating in Russia during the 1920s: the revolutionary *avant-garde* films, the foreign imports, and the domestically produced popular entertainments. Despite the cataclysmic changes that the revolution of 1917 wrought on both Russia and its film industry, though, the filmmakers of the new society didn't all begin from scratch. Several influential figures, such as Lev Kuleshev and Yakov Protazanov had begun their careers in the pre-revolutionary film industry – an industry whose cinema aesthetics are also in striking contrast to the montage aesthetics that continue dominate our conception of Russian silent cinema.

Before the Revolution

The film industry came late to pre-revolutionary Russia, but developed along reasonably standard lines. The French firms Pathè and Gaumont had been distributing films in Russia since around 1900 but in 1907 they opened a production centre in Moscow in response to competition from a native producer, and by the mid-1910s there was a range of producing firms, mainly centred in Moscow but also in Petrograd, Kiev and Odessa. Cinema exhibition also developed in this period, although again the main concentration of cinemas was in the major cities with little or no access to film for the vast rural and peasant populations who made up the majority of Russian citizens (see Youngblood 1999: 21). By 1914 a substantial industry existed, boasting star actors such as Ivan Mozzhukin and star directors, such as Yakov Protazonov and Yevgeni Bauer. The films themselves were highly distinctive, perhaps even baffling, in their narrative and aesthetic approaches. As Yuri Tsivian observes, 'a first encounter with Russian films of the 1910s can be puzzling; their stories seem to be moving at a wrong pace and in the wrong direction' (2003: 339). Tsivian identifies two unexpected characteristics of Russian films in this period; a tendency towards tragic endings, and an astonishingly slow pace – both of performance style and editing. He speculates about whether these characteristics might be considered somehow indicatively 'Russian'. Certainly the preference for tragic endings seems to accord with our conception of the 'Russian temperament' as established in nineteenth-century literature and theatre. Denise Youngblood even reports that the frequency of on-screen suicides in Russian cinema was matched by a fashion for committing suicide in the cinema auditorium itself (1999: 38–40). The audience preference for the sad ending seems to have been strong enough in Russia for film exporters to produce two endings to their films – a sad one for the domestic market, and a happy one for everywhere else. Tsivian, though, resists unverifiable speculations about the national temperament. Instead he points to the fact that tragic endings were actually quite common in the period before 1908, happy endings only becoming the norm as a result of a concerted campaign by American producers to distinguish their product from European imports. The Russian retention of the tragic ending, then, might be understood as either a holdover of earlier traditions, or a form of product differentiation (2003: 342).

The extraordinary formal qualities of the films might also be attributed to a kind of product differentiation. Anybody familiar with American films of the teens, particularly with the transformation in film language epitomised by D. W. Griffith's work at Biograph between 1908 and 1914 will be astounded by works of Yevgeni Bauer's such as *Twilight of a Woman's Soul* (1913) or *After Death* (1914). While Griffith's innovations of film technique emphasise editing and alterity in the establishment of space and the progression of narrative, Bauer's films work to a completely different principle. In Griffith's *A Girl and Her Trust* (1912) the relationship between the outer and the inner offices of the railway station are established early on by shots alternating between the two spaces, and cutting on the movement of characters through the door between the two rooms. A character in the outer office walks left to right, leaving the frame on the right-hand side, as he goes 'through' the door adjoining the offices. The image cuts to the inner office, with the character entering the frame on the left-hand side and closing the door behind him – still moving left to right. Continuity is ruthlessly established at the start, and maintained throughout so that later in the film when the heroine is locked in the inner office and the thieves are threatening her from the outer, the film can cut repeatedly between the two spaces without the viewer becoming disorientated. The heroine can even move across the inner office to the right – the side opposite the door leading back to the thieves – in order to telegraph for help to the next station using a machine positioned on the right extreme of the frame; and a cut to a further space – the station up the line – reveals an operator receiving her message from a machine wired up to the left of his frame, suggesting that the heroine is in the middle, with her attackers on the left and her colleague in the next station up the line to the right. Once these spatial relationships have been established, narrative and suspense effects can be produced simply by editing between the three spaces.

Bauer's films don't break these rules of continuity, but their emphasis is completely different. In the American film, the images within each frame are relatively flat – activity is organised along an axis from left to right, with the editing extending this dimension across three different spaces as though in a triptych. Shots are relatively brief – a few seconds at most – with meaning emerging from the juxtaposition of one shot with another. By contrast, in Bauer's films, individual shots are held for what seems (to an eye used to American cinema) to be an extraordinary amount of time. Often the scenes are arranged in depth, with narrative information emerging in the transitions of activity forward or back though the distant, middle and foreground of scenes elaborately laid out and lit to exploit and contrast these different depth fields. Careful blocking of actors and controlled lighting effects are designed to guide the eye of the viewer to primary narrative information within the scene, and editing rarely dissects space, or alternates between different spaces to suggest parallel actions. In fact these alternatives to the American system can be observed in other European cinema during the 1910s. David Bordwell eloquently describes the ways in which actors in the middle ground of scenes in Louis Feuillade's French crime serials *Fantomas* (1913) and *Les Vampires* (1915) adroitly and apparently casually step aside to reveal narratively significant figures or objects in the background, which then move forward to take centre stage (2005: 60). In the Italian diva film *Assunta Spina* (Gustavo Serena, 1912) the eponymous heroine (Francesca Bertini) attends the trial of her lover. The scene depicting the foyer of the courtroom is arranged to emphasise the axis leading from the foreground to the background where the doors into the courtroom itself are located in the centre of the frame. A desk is placed in the middle-ground on the left of the image, and another further back on the right, facing forward. Standing at the desk to the left, inspecting some papers, is the clerk of the court. At the opening of the shot he draws the eye, being the only figure in the frame, although there is nothing to indicate that he is anything other than an extra. The focus of our attention shifts as Assunta emerges from the courtroom doors at the back of the frame and proceeds towards the camera, surrounded by her retinue. Her lover has just been sentenced and she is distraught. As she passes the clerk we are reminded of his presence – their heads are close together in the frame and he moves his, looking up towards her and noticing her with interest. Immediately afterwards, he is obscured from our view by Assunta and her party who move directly in front of him, settling in the right foreground. Although most of the time our view of him is blocked by the figures of Assunta's retinue, we remain aware of him, staring intently at the scene unfolding – his face visible intermittently between the figures in the foreground. When Assunta's lover emerges from the courtroom being led away to prison, he and the gaolers move forward to occupy the right-hand foreground and interact with Assunta who stretches her arms out to him in lament. As he is led off to the right, followed by all the others except the heroine (who collapses back onto her chair), the clerk is once more revealed. He moves forward to make her his proposition...

This complex and sophisticated use of depth to produce a particular kind of narrative space, then, was already widespread in European cinema of the 1910s. But Bauer takes it to its most extreme conclusion in a series of celebrated *tours de force*, even extending this space by very early use of the camera dolly backwards or forwards. In *Twilight of a Woman's Soul*, Nina (Vera Dubovskaja) is a young noblewoman who is only roused from her *ennui* by a visit to the poor with her charitable mother. She resolves to devote her life to charitable work, but one of the working men she visits deceives her into returning to his lodgings alone, whereupon he rapes her. She kills him and slips away, distraught. Later, engaged to Prince Dol'skii, she feels compelled to warn him of her shameful past. 'I have belonged to another', she writes, but the letter cannot be delivered, and as a result it is only after they are married that she is able to confess. He is appalled. Retaining her dignity, she leaves him. He regrets his behaviour immediately and tries to find her. Years later, she has become a famous actress and he encounters her by chance. He asks her forgiveness but, in a scene reminiscent of *Eugene Onegin*, she rejects him. His apology is too late. He kills himself.

Yuri Tsivian highlights the extraordinary staging of the scene where the working man delivers the letter that deceives Nina into visiting him. It is staged in her bedroom, in a single shot, where lighting and furnishings have been arranged to delineate depth extremely clearly. In the background Nina sleeps in her bed, a lamp and a dressing table beside her to the right of the frame. The main expanse of the room in the middle-ground is uncluttered. Separating this space from the foreground is a translucent gauze curtain, which creates a sort of wash of light. The foreground is lit in such a way that objects and figures there appear in silhouette – two plant-stands and a chair and table, silhouetted, frame the scene beyond. To the right of the

Fig. 5: *Twilight of a Woman's Soul* (1913); deep staging – the intruder leaves a note on the table in the foreground, but can't resist creeping into the room to gaze at the sleeping heroine.

foreground on the frame-line is a window, the light from which, when the curtains are parted, pinpoints activity in the foreground. It is through this window that the man enters the scene, leaving his letter on the table where it remains highlighted in the crack of light through the curtains, the only lit object in the foreground.

Noticing Nina asleep beyond the gauze curtain, the man cannot help himself. He moves through into the middle ground, going from silhouette to fully-lit form, to gaze at her while she sleeps. His intruding presence is emphasised by three reflections that appear in the hinged mirror on the dressing table, as though not just one, but an army of intruders were threatening her. Fearful of waking her, he hastily retreats. She wakes and puts on a shawl, unaware of his having been there. We are constantly reminded of his recent presence, though, by the letter gleaming on the table in the foreground. She moves into the foreground, looking out of the window at the day as though part of her usual morning routine. We see the detail of her face as she draws back the curtains, and the light falls on it, so that when, finding the letter, she reads it, we can see her expression of astonishment and alarm. A single shot has been dressed and lit in such a way that an impressive range of narrative effects can be produced, without recourse to editing.

Perhaps the most audacious of Bauer's shots occurs in *After Death*, adapted from a story by Turgenev. It tells the story of another member of the aristocracy plagued by depression and *ennui*. Andre Bagrov (Vitold

Polonsky) has become a recluse after the death of his mother. His friend tries to rouse him with an invitation to a social gathering. Andre's alienating experience of the gathering is conveyed in a single remarkable shot lasting an astonishing three minutes – a miracle of choreography, not only of numbers of actors, but also of lighting and of camera movement. As Tsivian puts it, the staging seems designed 'to make us see how it feels to be trapped under the microscope of social curiosity' (2002). The camera follows Andre as his friend introduces him to what seems like an endless array of guests. Andre's alienation is emphasised by the camera movement which is the scene's most remarkable attribute. Steadily and very slowly it tracks backwards through the seemingly infinitely extendable space of the party as Andre is drawn left and right to greet new people. Fronds of foliage, curtains, pianos and ornamental pillars frame the image at strategic junctures only to recede further and further into the background as the scene continues its relentless course. The effect was apparently achieved by mounting the camera to two bicycles, but it is an audacious culmination of the tradition of creating narrative through depth-staging.

I have lingered over this phenomenon of pre-revolutionary Russian cinema partly because of the contrast it provides to other filmmaking techniques, particularly those emerging at this time in Hollywood, which were to become dominant, but also partly because of the contrast such film language offers to the montage effects that would become such a celebrated aspect of post-revolutionary Russian cinema. Bauer died unexpectedly of pneumonia only a few months before the Revolution. Other filmmakers chose to leave Russia when the crisis came to a head. Indeed, given the relentless emphasis on the niceties of social and moral behaviour among the aristocracy, and the tortured psychology of the supremely wealthy, coupled with the either completely uninterested or actively hostile portrayal of the poor in these films, it would be hard to imagine them finding favour with the new Bolshevik regime. The period's biggest star, Mozzhukhin, fled Russia at the end of the civil war in 1920 but continued to make films as an émigré in France, setting up a successful company which employed a number of refugees from the pre-revolutionary industry. Protazanov too, worked in France during the early 1920s, although he returned to the Soviet Union to make the science fiction fantasy *Aelita: Queen of Mars* (Yakov Protazanov, 1924).

Revolution and Civil War

On the face of it, Lenin's enthusiasm for cinema as an important tool of the Revolution seems well founded. Film was a modern, dynamic, genuinely mass medium, which was uniquely placed to address the diverse and scattered population of Russia's enormous landmass. Unlike literature or newspapers, it was accessible to the large percentage of Russians who remained illiterate, and unlike theatre it could be cheaply distributed – sent to the far corners of the country with the assurance that the films seen by the remotest audiences were the same as those seen in Moscow and Petrograd. In reality, though, filmmakers faced some daunting practical difficulties. On seizing power in October 1917, the Bolsheviks withdrew Russia from the First World War, but they were immediately thrown into a four-year civil war as the Red Army and the White Army (which was loyal to the previous regime) fought for overall control of the country. An economic blockade by other European powers and the cost of the civil war brought the country near to economic collapse, and Lenin introduced a policy of 'War Communism', which involved a range of emergency measures, nationalising industries and seizing private assets on an *ad hoc* basis. For filmmakers the primary problem was shortage of equipment and film stock. Those producers who had fled the regime had taken their cameras and other technical equipment with them. Since there were no native manufacturers of film cameras, projectors or even film stock, and the blockades meant that none could be imported, filmmakers were left with aging equipment and nothing to film on. Cinemas had to re-run old pre-revolutionary films, no matter how worn or familiar. As projection equipment wore out, spare parts were impossible to locate (see Kepley 1991: 65). The cinemas themselves were in a deplorable condition, and anyway there were relatively few of them outside Moscow and Petrograd. Youngblood cites a British journalist reporting that as late as 1922 only 90 of the 143 cinemas in Moscow were operational. She quotes his description of one of them, whose 'decorated ceiling had been newly decorated by shot and shell and had a special ventilation system introduced by the method of dropping eggs from aeroplanes' (1992: 15).

What little film stock could be obtained was used in producing short newsreels such as those made by Dziga Vertov, which were sent out around the country in specially converted trains. These now famous 'agit-trains' were equipped with generators, old pre-war projectors and seating, to operate as mobile cinemas, although operators might also take their projector into a town or village square to set up an open-air show. The newsreels produced by Vertov during this 1918–19 period – the *Kino-week* series – are relatively conventional in form, showing public events and speeches, military leaders in the civil war, the repatriation of German prisoners of war, celebrations of industrial or agricultural achievements, etc.[1] In later series, such as *Kino Pravda* (Dziga Vertov, 1922–25), Vertov introduced more formal experimentation, such as running the film backwards to show the process of bread baking – the loaf returning to wheat in the fields. Vertov also experimented with dynamic titling and montage effects, his work culminating in the extraordinary feature-length documentary masterpiece *Man With a Movie Camera*, which combined a range of different editing, superimposition and rhythmic techniques into a dazzling 'city symphony'. For Vertov, the early experience of showing films to remote audiences who had never experienced film before was to affect his entire conception of cinema. He claimed that these 'unspoiled viewers' responded much more readily to documentary and actuality footage than to conventional drama films – films he dismissed as 'toxic'. Peasant audiences, he recalled in 1926, inspected the urgent agitational posters decorating the trains not for their political messages, but for their accuracy and relevance to their own lives. They dismissed the horses they saw represented as 'horse actors' because their shoes were incorrectly drawn. The same happened, he claimed, with fictional films:

> A 'lady' remains a lady to them, no matter what 'peasant clothing' you show her in. These viewers ... still don't understand the taste of film-moonshine, and when, after the sugary actors of a drama, real peasants appear on the screen, they all perk up and stare at the screen.
>
> A real tractor, which these viewers know of only from hearsay, has plowed over a few acres in a matter of minutes, before their very eyes. Conversations, shouts, questions. There's no question of actors. On the screen are their own kind, real people. There isn't a single false, theatrical moment to unmask the screen, to shake the peasants' confidence. (1992: 61)

Later Vertov refined his ideas about the way in which cinema could achieve the truth of 'life caught unawares', celebrating the camera as a mechanism 'more perfect than the human eye' both because of its indifference to emotion, and its ability – through editing – to express *and create* a new world. Crucially, he suggested, this act of creation would happen through montage – through cutting different images together to produce a new whole. 'I am kino-eye. I am a builder', he wrote, elegiacally in 1923. The camera, he suggested could create a 'perfect man' by cutting together images of hands, legs, heads from different people. Or a new city, or a new time plane, or an entirely new event:

> You're walking down a Chicago street in 1923, but I make you greet Comrade Volodarsky, walking down a Petrograd street in 1918, and he returns your greeting.
>
> Another example: the coffins of national heroes are lowered into the grave (shot in Astrakhan in 1918); the grave is filled in (Kronstadt, 1921); cannon salute (Petrograd, 1920); memorial service, hats are removed (Moscow, 1922) – such things go together, even with thankless footage not specifically shot for this purpose (cf. *Kinopravda* no. 13). The montage of crowds and of machines greeting Comrade Lenin (*Kinopravda* no. 14), filmed in different places at different times, belongs in this category. (1992: 16)

Vertov was not the only Soviet filmmaker to recognise the creative power of film editing. Given the difficulty of filming new material due to the shortage of film stock, it seems hardly surprising that numerous film-makers of the period turned their attention to the possibilities presented by editing for creating new meanings from old materials. The most famous example is that of Lev Kuleshov who had started his career as a scene-builder for Yevgeni Bauer. By 1919 he was teaching at the Moscow Film School, and the famous experiment which bears his name was precisely the result of re-editing old footage left over from the pre-revolutionary cinema in order to see how new meanings emerged. Kuleshov took a single strip of film showing the face of the pre-revolutionary star, Mozzhukhin. Into this shot he spliced an image of a bowl of soup, then of a corpse in a coffin, then of a reclining woman. When the results were shown to audiences they interpreted Mozzhukhin's face according to the image accompanying it –

creating a connection between the two images which expressed not just spatial proximity (they thought the actor was 'looking' at each object), but also emotional response. When Mozzhukhin 'looked' at the soup they interpreted hunger in his face, when he 'looked' at the corpse they saw grief, and when he 'looked' at the woman, they saw lust. Meaning emerged not simply from the images themselves, Kuleshov concluded, but from the association of different images when edited together – an association that was supplied by the audience in attempting to interpret the relationship of one image to another.

Kuleshov created many other similar experiments of editing effects, including the 'creative man' and the 'creative geography' experiments that Vertov draws on in his writing, quoted above (see Yampolsky 1991: 45). Importantly, he showed that the audience continues to interpret images in juxtaposition, even when none of the careful cues of editing associated with the American 'continuity system' are present. That is to say, that if a filmmaker using the continuity system were to film a scene of a man looking at soup, they would be careful to build a range of continuity 'cues' into the two images to suggest that they were connected. If the shot of the actor showed him looking down towards the soup, the answering shot of the soup bowl would have to be filmed from an angle roughly matching the actor's eye-line – the camera would have to be looking down on the soup as the actor had been. If behind the actor there was wallpaper visible covering the walls of the room, the room in which the soup was filmed would have the same wallpaper to make it clear that the actor and the soup were in the same space. Similarly the lighting would have to be consistent across the shots, with light coming from the 'right' direction, depending on the exact special relationship being suggested by the two shots. Kuleshov's images had none of these 'cues'. Indeed they had been filmed at completely separate times in separate spaces by separate filmmakers – they were just random old bits of found footage, but the simple act of editing them together was *enough* to create meaning. Among Kuleshov's students and colleagues at the film school were directors who went on to develop and refine these ideas, testing the boundaries of what could be done through montage, and creating some of the most canonical films of the Soviet period – indeed some of the most canonical films of cinema itself. Films such as Sergei Eisenstein's *Battleship Potemkin* and *Strike* (1925), Vsevolod Pudovkin's *Mother* (1926) and *The End of St Petersburg* (1927),

Alexander Dovzhenko's *Arsenal* (1929) and *Earth* (1930) didn't just have montage in common, though. They also shared an absolute commitment to the idea of cinema as an agitational, revolutionary, galvanising art form, whose purpose is not simply to entertain its audience, but to educate it – to raise it to a political and revolutionary consciousness by revealing to it the process of history. Kracauer, commenting on Lubitsch's German historical epics such as *Madam Dubarry*, chastised Lubitsch for denying historical process, replacing it with psychological motivations of invented or re-imagined characters:

> Instead of tracing all revolutionary events to their economic and ideal causes, [the film] persistently presents them as the outcome of psychological conflicts. It is a deceived lover who, animated by the desire for retaliation, talks the masses into capturing the Bastille. Similarly, Madame du Barry's execution is related not so much to political reasons as to the motives of personal revenge. [The film] does not exploit the passions inherent in the Revolution, but reduces the Revolution to a derivative of private passions. (1947: 49)

Emphatically this is a trap that Soviet filmmakers did not to fall into. Their films were structured around the idea of history as a series of revolutionary processes and relationships. They focused on incidents and events – usually in the recent history of the Soviet revolution itself – which were then relentlessly traced to their 'economic and ideal causes'. In Eisenstein's work in particular, individual psychology – indeed individual characters – were downplayed in favour of narratives that foregrounded and explained the relationships between bodies of people, classes and institutions. *Strike*, for instance, tells the story of a strike in a Moscow factory at the turn of the century, a fictional compendium of the increasing number of incidents of unrest and suppression that preceded the Bolshevik uprising. In the film we do not follow the story of the strike as it affects a main protagonist, or indeed a family. Some characters appear recurrently, but they are only offered as symbols of wider experiences and events. The emphasis is instead on describing the processes of the strike as a whole and the methods of the individual groups and forces involved – a style which Yuri Tsivian has described as 'production analysis' (2000).

Early in the film we are shown numerous scenes of the workers in secret meetings in a variety of locations, each chosen because it is confusing and difficult for the foreman to find and infiltrate. We are also shown the way in which the manager and owner of the factory respond to rumours of impending strike action, and the methods of various secret police agents recruited to spy on the workers. Montage editing contributes to and emphasises this effect – the *avant-garde* method is closely related to the agitational intention of the film. Because we are not allied to any one character's psychology, we are also not allied to the smooth expression of a protagonist's visual point of view. Literally, the camera is free to view the action from any angle. Similarly, the concern always to orientate the viewer in time and space is abandoned in favour of a search for striking shots offering graphic contrasts, visual clashes and eloquent symbolism.

That such editing may prove disorientating only contributes to the intended effect – to galvanise and energise the audience to action. Spatial disorientation is often introduced deliberately – cutting between two shots of the same action optically reversed such as with the images of the priest in the early section of *Battleship Potemkin*, for instance, or suddenly cutting away from the climax of an action to a series of symbolic close-ups before returning to the primary action.

The film is an account of a real mutiny which occurred in 1905, an act of resistance to imperial rule and worker exploitation, a precursor to the events of 1918. In an early scene the sailors refuse to eat the rotten meat provided for them, and stand on deck facing a firing squad for their insubordination. In the moments between the Captain's order for the firing squad to 'take aim' and the order to 'fire', Eisenstein shows us a rhythmically-timed series of close-ups, none of which are motivated by any single character's point of view or even proximity. Faces of the watching sailors, the officers, a detail of the captain's fingers stroking his sword hilt, his head turning to give the order, the mutineers' knees dropping to the deck, a row of officers' legs, the firing squad in a row of aiming rifles, another row of rifles aiming in the opposite direction across the frame, Valkulinchuk – the leader of the mutiny, the firing squad, a close-up of the priest's crucifix in his hand, a lifebelt bearing the name of the ship, the prow of the ship seen from below bearing the Imperial crest, a bugle resting in the hands of the bugler, the sailors falling to their knees, Valkulinchuk again. All of these shots are close-ups of a few moments duration at the

Figs. 6, 7 & 8: *Strike* (1925); montage – numerous shots cut together to express a single brief incident; the foreman is knocked over by a wheel.

most, the entire sequence lasts less than thirty seconds. Eisenstein has extended the moment of maximum tension to convey the agonising sense of time standing still, but also incorporated a series of symbolic images – the crucifix, the lifebelt, the crest on the prow of the ship – to remind the audience of the wider political significance of the battle of wills taking place on deck. In other examples, we can see Eisenstein using similar techniques to both extend time and to introduce associative symbolic imagery. In *Strike* an incident showing a foreman being knocked down by a massive wheel that is dangling from a moving crane in the factory is conveyed using as many as ten separate angles on the moment of impact, edited together in swift succession to extend the impact of the moment on the viewer.

David Bordwell describes this technique as 'overlapping editing', arguing that it 'creates a nervous, vibrating rhythm and allows [Eisenstein] to rearrange elements from shot to shot' (2003: 373). In the celebrated climax of the film, the massacre of the strikers is intercut with non-diegetic images of a bull being slaughtered in an abattoir – an image which the director claimed would function to 'stir the spectator to a state of pity and terror which would be unconsciously and automatically transferred to the shooting of the strikers' (quoted in Bordwell 2003: 386).

The New Economic Policy and Soviet Cinema

The Soviet montage films swiftly took on iconic status, particularly within the intellectual film community. Directors such as Kuleshov, Eisenstein and Pudovkin wrote their theories about filmmaking, which were translated and published in international journals such as *Close Up*. *Strike, Potemkin* and *Mother* were initially banned from exhibition in Britain owing to their political content, but such was their reputation that the London Film Society (founded as a subscription club precisely in order to circumvent such censorship) fought to show them. They finally secured *Potemkin* in 1927, by which time its reputation as a masterwork was already assured.

These *avant-garde* films were less well received by ordinary Russians, though. Denise J. Youngblood suggests that most of them ran for only a week or less in first-run theatres (1992: 18). Ironically, their production was indirectly reliant on a different kind of international cinema culture, and a different kind of editing. The end of the civil war in 1921 signalled also the end of the emergency measures and hardships of Lenin's War Communism, and the recognition that it would have to be replaced with a new strategy focused on economic recovery through growth and investment. This 'New Economic Policy' (NEP) was launched as a temporary measure, designed to attract enough growth and investment to enable the country to become self-sufficient once more. Thus, while the Government retained ultimate control, a limited return to private ownership and market competition was encouraged. Furthermore, the international blockade on trade with the Soviets was lifted and trade negotiations were opened with the British and others from 1921, relieving the shortage of film stock and technical equipment. Vance Kepley stresses the control the Government still exerted over such trading relationships – all imports and exports were channelled through a central government agency, which carefully monitored the balance of trade and was thus able to 'arrange for surpluses in one sector to offset deficits in another' (1991: 72). In this way, Kepley suggests, the weak film industry was able to benefit from the strength of agricultural exports due to good harvests and high grain prices throughout the 1920s. In film terms, this meant that from 1922 popular foreign films could be imported from abroad in order to generate revenues at the box office that could then be invested in restoring cinemas themselves, and in reviving the domestic film industry. Some attempts were also made to attract direct foreign investment in the production industry. These met with limited success since the precariousness of the industry's position made it unattractive to foreign investors. One exception to this rule was the company Mezhrabpom, which benefitted from extensive investment through the Worker's International Relief Fund, a socialist organisation based in Germany. The company concentrated on producing populist dramas and comedies that would do well at the box office, and this successful policy was also adopted by other companies once the profits generated from foreign imports could be put into production (see Kepley 1991: 70). Thus, when Lenin referred to the 'worthless film ... of a more or less usual type' which might have to be shown along with propaganda shorts in order 'to attract the public', he could have meant one of two different kinds of production – a foreign import, probably from Hollywood, or a domestically-produced film which downplayed ideological concerns in favour of genre pleasures and entertainment values.

Having been starved of new films for several years, audiences immediately responded to the foreign films that began to be imported from 1921 onwards. Youngblood shows the numbers of imported films rose rapidly to a peak of over three hundred in 1924–25, and then fell off almost as rapidly as domestic production began to catch up, before these also petered out at the end of the decade due to the difficulties of the transition to sound and the shift in film policy under Stalin. During the mid-1920s, though, it was largely Hollywood productions that ruled the box office and dominated the cinemas. As she points out, even when domestic productions outnumbered imports towards the end of the decade, it was still the imports that triumphed at the box office and dominated the first-run cinemas. Not all imports were from Hollywood. The German comedian Harry Piel was particularly popular with Soviet audiences. Nevertheless the biggest stars of the USA were also the biggest draws in the USSR, with Mary Pickford and Douglas Fairbanks the top favourites. Youngblood estimates that Fairbanks' vehicle *The Thief of Baghdad* (Raoul Walsh, 1924) was the biggest hit of the decade (1992: 20).

It seems astonishing to consider that at the same time *Battleship Potemkin* was completely banned from the UK because of its political ideology, the Soviet Government was actively importing popular American films. What, one wonders, did Soviet audiences who had been enduring the hardships of 'War Communism' for the previous four years, make of Hollywood films like *It* (Clarence Badger, 1927) or *Orchids and Ermine* (Alfred Santell, 1927), which absolutely celebrate American values of capitalism, individualism and commodity consumption. In fact, of course, although some imported films were deemed innocuous enough to be shown in their original form, most films were extensively re-edited in order to shift the ideological emphasis towards a more acceptably Soviet interpretation of class relations. Re-editing in this way was one of the crucial ways in which the discoveries made by Kuleshov about the power of montage to create new meanings from existing material were put to use, and indeed such re-editing work formed a key part of the training of filmmakers themselves (see Tsivian 1996).

An excellent example of such practices is provided by the recent discovery in the Moscow film archives of a British production previously thought lost. *Three Live Ghosts* (George Fitzmaurice, 1922) was an adaptation of a successful stage play, made in London by the American company Paramount as part of its short-lived policy of producing in the UK. Its primary source of interest is that it is one of the earliest films on which a youthful Alfred Hitchcock worked. An interest in Hitchcock is what led Charles Barr to seek it out, and to discover the only extant version to be an ex-distribution print held in Moscow, which had indeed been re-edited to suit Soviet ideologies. The original story can be reconstructed from the play, synopses in British trade papers and reviews, etc. It concerns three soldiers returning from the First World War, only to discover that they have been officially recorded as dead and must, for various comic and bureaucratic reasons, remain so. One of the three pals is an aristocrat who is suffering from amnesia. The film, then, immediately presented two ideological problems, as recorded in the report of the Moscow censor, which found that 'the picture is completely harmful and unacceptable, given the way it interprets the consequences of the world war and the way it agitates for the social friendship of hostile classes...' (quoted in Barr, forthcoming). Although the initial recommendation was that the film should be banned, it was eventually re-edited. Barr offers a detailed analysis of just how extensive and successful the re-edit was, excising almost all reference to the war, and reframing the story to be about three down-and-outs, identified through a didactic opening section as victims of the capitalist system. The aristocratic character is also changed into an opera singer down on his luck, with the scenes showing his palatial home transformed into scenes showing him visiting the opera house. As Barr points out, the lessons of the Kuleshov experiment are put to thorough use throughout this process.

Whether re-edited or not, the imported films proved extremely popular with audiences. Hollywood stars – with all the connotations of glamorous consumption that they embodied – were worshipped by Soviet filmgoers. This taste for American films and stars caused much disquiet for some commentators, who saw in it evidence of the 'extraordinary decadence and poor taste of the youth and the public of the third balcony' – as Lev Kuleshov put it in his article on 'Americanitis'. Kuleshov did not share this opinion himself, but rather argued that American films should be studied by Russian filmmakers, in an attempt to discover what it was about them that commanded such a broad appeal (see Youngblood 1992: 50). Action and pace were qualities that Kuleshov identified as being particularly appealing to audiences, as well as a tendency toward happy endings. The craze for American stars reached its climax in July 1926 with the visit to Moscow of Hollywood's 'royal couple', Douglas Fairbanks and Mary Pickford. Crowds lined the streets to greet them, and the newsreels covered their every move. These scenes formed the basis for one of Soviet cinema's most delightful domestic productions, *A Kiss from Mary Pickford* (Sergey Komarov, 1927). The film successfully and self-consciously imitates the style of American films while both celebrating and critiquing the craze for them among young fans. It opens with a vision of its heroine, Duzya (Anel Sudakevich) frantically emoting into the camera. Her look of passionate desire turns to one of astonishment, then anger, and then fury as she waves her fists at an imaginary assailant and finally drops into her chair in a dead faint. She is training, it seems, to become a movie star, but her tutor is not impressed – he doesn't think she's put enough 'feeling' in to her performance. Later as she scribbles Zorro moustachios on a photograph in her notebook, a classmate asks her who the picture is of. 'Oh,' she responds, giving herself the airs of a *bona fide* star, 'only one of my many admirers!'

Her admirer is actually Goga (played by the comedian Igor Ilyinsky, perhaps the biggest domestic star of the era), and we are introduced to him next, working as an usher, tearing tickets at the local cinema. He admires Duzya so much that he is too busy kissing her photograph to notice a schoolboy sneaking into the cinema behind him. Although his shift is ending, he doesn't plan to go home, as he has a date to take Duzya into the cinema. Duzya, though, treats him with complete distain. She sends him off to change out of his usher's uniform before she will consent to be seen with him, and while he's away she spots the man she *really* cares for – Douglas Fairbanks – whose image in numerous posters and publicity stills advertising *The Mask of Zorro* (Fred Niblo, 1920) adorn the walls of the cinema foyer. Like Goga before her, she passionately kisses the photographic image of her love. *He* is her real date, and without waiting for Goga she slips into the cinema to be with him. Later, transported by the vision of Fairbanks enfolding his heroine in a screen kiss, Duzya is appalled to find that the man sitting with her is not her hero, but only Goga. 'You're not a superstar!' she declares – she will only consent for him to accompany her home once he's famous. Trying to impress her, Goga transforms himself into Fairbanks at a party, with hilarious, though disastrous, results (Ilyinsky offering a brilliant parody of Fairbanks' distinctively bouncy performance style). Later, of course, he achieves film stardom as a result of having been filmed being kissed by Mary Pickford on her visit to the studios where he is working as a stuntman – the shot one of several cut into the film from the newsreel coverage of the actual visit of Pickford and Fairbanks. Once the magical star status has been bestowed on him, though, he and Duzya find that it isn't all it's cracked up to be. The couple are mobbed and pestered to distraction by adoring fans desperate to be close to them.

This gentle critique offers a reminder that while popular domestic films often capitalised on the benefits of the New Economic Policy, they were still careful to distance themselves from the new class which it was popularly considered to have encouraged. In *Bed and Sofa* there is a hint of criticism of the characters and their attachment to material objects, particularly of Liuda and her fascination with film stars. *The Girl with a Hatbox* (Boris Barnet, 1927) satirises the greed and selfishness of 'NEPmen' (capitalists who have profited from the new policy). The employers of Natasha (Anna Sten) run a millinery business in Moscow. Greedy for extra space, they have registered her as a resident of their house, even though she lives outside Moscow with her grandfather. In order to maintain the fiction of her residency to the authorities, they ask her to stay at least a night or two in the house, and Natasha responds by marrying a young student in need of accommodation so that he acquires the right to use the room instead, much to the comic consternation and outrage of the greedy 'NEP' couple. Increasingly though, as the NEP gave way to Stalin's 'Cultural Revolution' in the late 1920s, such films began to be attacked on ideological grounds as not critical *enough* of policies that were now falling out of favour (see Youngblood 1992: 137). Foreign films stopped being imported into the USSR at the end of the silent period, and a new style of domestic production emerged in the 1930s.

Note

1   Issues can be viewed online at the Austrian film museum website: http://www.filmmuseum.at/en/collections/film_collection/film_online/kinonedelja_online_edition

4   AMERICA – CONTINUITY AND DOMINANCE

Cinema has its own group styles; German Expressionism [and]
Soviet montage cinema ... afford time-honoured instances. But to
suggest that Hollywood cinema constitutes a group style seems
more risky. In other national schools, a handful of filmmakers
worked within sharply contained historical circumstances for only
a few years. But Hollywood, as an extensive commercial enterprise,
included hundreds of filmmakers and thousands of films... If it is
a daunting challenge to define a German Expressionist cinema ...
it might seem impossible to circumscribe a distinctive Hollywood
'group style'.
　　　　　– David Bordwell, *Classical Hollywood Cinema* (1988: 3)

In Chapters Two and Three I attempted to challenge the idea that German
cinema can be understood purely through recourse to 'expressionism'
and that Russian cinema can be considered coterminous with Soviet
'montage' during the 1920s. I have emphasised the status of German
and Russian cinema as commercial enterprises (even in the case of the
Soviets), encompassing a wide variety of popular styles and genres and
involving many more than just a 'handful' of filmmakers. That is not to
say that those 'group styles' didn't exist, of course. As we have seen, they
were extremely important for the international visibility and circulation
of these cinemas within intellectual film culture. Rather, it is to suggest

that such 'group styles' might best be regarded as useful starting points – seductive brands that serve to draw the researcher towards a particular national cinema, but ultimately also encourage a wider investigation of the diverse cinematic pleasures to be found there, beyond the most obvious examples. Nevertheless, as David Bordwell argues above, Hollywood cinema presents an entirely different set of definition problems – problems that arise not so much from the uniqueness of Hollywood film style, but rather from its consistency, its longevity and its *dominance*. Throughout the 1920s, one could argue, Hollywood filmmaking dominated the cinema markets of Europe and America, both in terms of its style and in terms of its economic and industrial clout. In many ways the dominance of Hollywood filmmaking was the background against which European 'group styles' defined themselves. The lighting and stylised *mise-en-scène* of expressionism was noticeable *because* of the way in which it departed from Hollywood's naturalistic lighting and composition conventions. Montage editing in Russian films seemed shocking and exciting *because* it broke the rules associated with the American continuity system. Industrially too, Hollywood offered an ever-present alternative. As we have seen, when Germany and the USSR opened their markets to foreign product, it was Hollywood films that proved most popular with audiences, and Hollywood firms that had the financial muscle to make good the opportunities that foreign markets presented – as, for instance, with the Parufamet agreement in Germany. The situation was even more pronounced in Britain, where a tradition of free trade and a shared language made the domestic market particularly vulnerable to the popularity of American films and the aggressiveness of US business practices. Above all, partly as a result of their 'style', Hollywood films were *popular*. Throughout the 1920s, articles can be found in the British trade press urging filmmakers to compete with American filmmakers by emulating the efficiency of their style. In order to achieve the popularity of Hollywood films, they suggested, British films should be more narratively focused, they should be faster both in their plotting and in their editing, they should address a 'universal' audience by focusing on ordinary people and classless situations, and finally they should feature really charismatic stars.

What were the reasons behind the extraordinary dominance of Hollywood cinema, then, and what was it about the films that made them so universally popular with audiences, not just in the USA but also across the world? In this chapter I shall address these questions, as well as offering an account of the ways in which Hollywood films responded to some of the key social and cultural changes occurring in American culture during the 1920s. As Bordwell suggests, the sheer size of the output of Hollywood during this period, and the wealth of well-known films, make selection quite difficult. I have chosen to focus in particular on the ways in which women were involved in the industry, both as producers and as consumers of film texts, and also on the question of how Hollywood filmmakers portrayed ideas about American citizenship itself onscreen, through stories of immigration and aspiration.

Industrial consolidation

Some initial clues as to the reasons behind Hollywood's dominance can be found simply by considering the geography and history of the USA. The sheer size of the country ensured a massive domestic market, more profitable than anything that was possible in European producing nations. The film industry emerged just as the USA was going through a period of rapid industrialisation, and a transformation of business practices across the board to reflect a 'modern' business science that emphasised efficiency, planning and integration. Hand in hand with this development was an increasing tendency for business concerns to combine into 'trusts' or to merge with each other, ensuring market pre-eminence by simply absorbing their competitors, and promoting vertical and horizontal efficiency savings by acquiring companies that offered ancillary services. The many small production companies that had competed at the turn of the century initially came together as the Motion Picture Patents Company (MPPC) in 1908 under pressure from Thomas Edison, who controlled the patents for much of the camera and projector equipment in the USA. The effect of this combination was to enable a certain amount of standardisation within the industry, but also to squeeze out competitors who were not members of the trust. As Richard Abel has argued, around 1910 the MPPC was instrumental in engineering a shift away from European imports, particularly French Pathé films that had previously dominated the US market (but which began to be characterised as 'unwholesome') and towards domestic films characterised as 'healthy' and 'American' – particularly early westerns (1999: 151). Although the MPPC did not survive into the 1920s, the pattern involving a small group of film companies co-operating to protect the interests of the industry as a whole and to exclude competitors remained an essential element of Hollywood's oligopoly structure. Vertical integration also ensured efficiencies across the production and distribution process. Major companies of the 1920s such as Paramount or Metro-Goldwyn-Mayer not only owned the large studios where films were made, they also owned the distribution organisation, as well as the networks of cinemas across the country where the films were shown. Thus, box office revenue could be ploughed straight back into production without any independent middlemen syphoning off the profits. Because of the size of the market and the incredible demand for product from the theatres, producers had to develop ways of creating large numbers of films extremely quickly and efficiently. Most cinemas from 1910 onwards changed their programme at least twice a week meaning that producers had to have a steady supply of new films to satisfy audience demand. Here again, the business innovations of the period had a role to play. Much like the Ford assembly-line system, filmmaking in Hollywood became marked by standardisation of product, and specialisation of labour. Developing throughout the 1910s, this tendency reached its maturity around 1914 with what Janet Staiger calls the 'central producer system'. Under this system each task – from scriptwriting to directing to costume design to lighting to editing to marketing – became the responsibility of specialist departments who worked on that particular activity for each film produced. Hand in hand with this specialisation came standardisation, which ensured that each scriptwriter, or lighting technician or editor, performed their task according to a predetermined standard – a certain quality, but also according to certain stated rules to ensure a consistent look and feel to the films produced. Staiger emphasises the important role of the continuity script in this process. The script offered a kind of blueprint for the film, which could be passed along to each department of the studio in order to ensure the smooth and efficient co-ordination of every element. As Staiger states:

> A written script which included descriptions of each shot and its adjacent shots provided a long-term cost advantage. It was cheaper to pay a few workers to prepare scripts and solve continuity problems at that stage than it was to let a whole crew of laborers work it out on set or by retakes later. (1988: 138)

Even before 1914, then, the American film industry had achieved an efficiency and a dominance that was not matched by its more *ad hoc* European rivals. The First World War enhanced this effect as Hollywood continued to produce and export while European filmmakers were increasingly turning inward, their export ambitions stagnating as a result of the hostilities. Perhaps most importantly, after the war, while most European economies teetered on the brink of collapse, America reaped the benefits of the new business methods with an unprecedented period of manufacturing and consumer prosperity. Rising wages and falling prices produced the 'jazz age', a consumer society such as had never been seen before, and Hollywood cinema – with its emphasis on aspiration, pleasure, consumption, glamour, fashion and *stars* – operated as its perfect shop window.

Continuity Editing – Standardisation and Variation

What was the style that got standardised through this process, and why did it prove so appealing to audiences? Like the British trade commentators mentioned above, Bordwell identifies *narrative* as the primary concern of Hollywood cinema, emphasising the extent to which its systems are devoted to conveying stories in a clear and unambiguous way. Bordwell also notes that in doing this, Hollywood films strive to 'conceal their artifice' – they do not draw attention to the way in which they are put together, but instead seek to ensure that audiences, by remaining orientated in time and space and focused on the story, forget that they are interpreting a complex series of flat, mute, moving pictures, and instead imagine themselves in a three-dimensional fiction world (1988: 1–70). One of the key methods for achieving this is through continuity editing.

In the previous chapter I discussed an early example of the continuity editing style demonstrated in Griffith's *A Girl and Her Trust*. I described how the relationship between different spaces in the film is rigorously established at the start of the film by a series of edits which show characters moving from one room to another through a door situated on the frame-line, using an edit-on-action carefully placed at the moment they move through the door. A continuous action from left to right is extended by the edit, as they pass out of the right-hand side of the frame into the left-hand side of the next frame which depicts the room on the other

Figs. 9, 10 & 11: *The Unseen
Enemy* (1912); continuity
editing – consistency of
camera position enables clear
orientation within space;
the relationship between the
individual shots creates the
narrative space.

side of the 'door'. Having established the spatial layout at the beginning of his film, Griffith is able to create narrative tension simply by cutting between the various spaces – the thieves doing their dastardly work in the first room while the heroine, having locked herself in the second room, telegraphs for help. Another example of this rigorous system can be seen in Griffith's *The Unseen Enemy* (1912). Again, middle-class women (and the property they are entrusted with) are under threat from working-class thieves. Here, two sisters (Dorothy and Lillian Gish) are locked in the room on the right, while a drunken servant and her companion attempt to blow open a safe containing the girls' inheritance in the room on the left. Griffith is able to cut between the terrified girls and the villains – creating tension and narrative simply in the act of editing between the two spaces. Griffith extends the action when one of the girls uses a telephone to call for help and we cut to a further space where her brother, on the other end of the phone, is alerted to their plight. When the thieving maid fires a gun through a hole in the wall, forcing the girl to drop the phone, the brother is appalled, and races home to the rescue.

Tom Gunning has commented on the efficiency of these films, not only in the way their editing relentlessly drives the narrative forward, but also in the way the narrative relies on patriarchal bourgeois values which associate the working classes with threat, women with property and the domestic sphere, and men with heroism and action. They also, he notes, respond to ambivalent ideas about modernity, frequently featuring new technologies of transport and communication, such as the motorcar and the telephone, which act both as sources of comfort (closing distance, eradicating danger), and anxiety (for instance, when they break down at crucial moments or when, as in *The Unseen Enemy*, they emphasise the hero's helplessness) (1990: 336; 1991: 184).

The primary interest of a film such as *The Unseen Enemy*, though, derives from the narrative tension, created through what came to be known as 'parallel editing' – cutting back and forth between shots showing action happening simultaneously in a variety of different spaces – the sisters in increasing peril, the threatening villains, the brother's frantic efforts to return and rescue them. The success of this technique is entirely dependent on the audiences' orientation – their clear understanding about where and when each action is taking place. This is established and reinforced at the beginning of the film and throughout by the consistency of the framing and the editing. Griffith's work at the Biograph company between 1908 and 1914 (during which he produced over 450 such short narratives) is often understood to embody the advances in editing techniques that later became standardised as the 'continuity system'. It is certainly a reputation Griffith was happy to cultivate for himself, taking out an advertisement in the *New York Dramatic Mirror* in 1913 to claim the invention of not only parallel editing, but also of the close-up, the establishing shot, restrained acting and the fade-out.

Nevertheless, Griffith was not the only contributor to the 'transformation of cinema' during the 1910s. In recent years it has been increasingly acknowledged that he must take his place among a whole host of filmmakers whose different solutions to continuity problems – some of which became standard practice and others of which remained dead ends – cumulatively contributed to the emergence of the editing and framing conventions with which we are still familiar today. Lois Weber, for instance, working for the Rex Motion Picture Company during the same period, was just as prolific in her output of short narratives. Her *Suspense* (1913) is worth considering in comparison with the Griffith films mentioned above. Here again is the familiar situation – a woman alone in an isolated house is beset by an intruding tramp while her husband, alerted to her plight by a telephone call, is helpless to assist. Shelley Stamp suggests that Weber may even have made the film as an explicit response to Griffith's famous examples (2015: 42). At the start of the film the spatial configuration of the rooms in the house is again made explicit through editing – although the strategies used are different to those of Griffith. A maid in the back kitchen prepares to leave, writing a note explaining that she cannot bear to remain in the lonesome spot a moment longer. She looks to the right of the frame, where – as in *The Unseen Enemy* and *A Girl and Her Trust* – there is a door leading to the inner room. But instead of reinforcing this relationship by walking through the door, she peers through the keyhole, and Weber shows us her *point of view*, a close-up – through a keyhole-shaped mask – of the heroine tending her young baby in the inner room. Later, another point of view shot affords us a spectacular moment of terror when the heroine, leaning out of an upstairs window, looks down and comes face to face for the first time with the tramp. Shot from her position directly above his head, the image shows him stop, twist his face upwards, and leer directly into the camera. Weber renders the telephone conversation between husband and wife, not through editing as Griffith had done, but through a split-screen device, with the husband in the middle of the screen, and his wife on the right-hand side, while the tramp she can hear is shown prowling around on the left. The device may look unusual to modern audiences compared to Griffith's solution, but it still re-enforces the spatial dynamic of the film established in the opening scene, since the wife is telephoning from the inner room (on the right) and the tramp is about to enter the kitchen to the left. Weber's film is a good example of the variety of solutions to continuity problems that the Hollywood system allowed, even while continuing to insist on the absolute orientation of the viewer within the fictional space. As Stamp suggests, they also have an ideological function: 'One might even suggest that the unusual camera angles so often noted in *Suspense* become a means of destabilising the logic enforced by parallel editing, skewing the strict binarism that had come to characterise so many race-to-the-rescue films' (ibid.).

Alice Guy's *Making an American Citizen* (1912) provides a third example of the editing styles that fed into the continuity system. Guy, like Weber and Griffith, produced an enormous number of short films on a very quick turnover during her time as the chief filmmaker and artistic director of the Solax film company. She had started her career in France with the Gaumont Company, and was thus herself a recent immigrant to the USA. *Making an American Citizen* tells the semi-humorous story of an immigrant couple arriving in America from Russia. Ivan Orloff is shown mistreating his wife. When they are in their native Russia he treats her no better than their donkey – literally hitching her to a cart and forcing her to pull it alongside the animal as he whips them both. On their arrival in America Ivan is taught five 'lessons in Americanism'. In a series of vignettes, upright American citizens intervene to prevent Ivan's mistreatment of his wife, violently punishing him for his 'un-American' behaviour. Finally, he is sentenced to four months penal servitude as a punishment for beating her, and this lesson, meted out not by concerned neighbours but with the full force of the State, finally produces a reformation. The final scene shows Ivan reconciled with his wife, and fully endorsing American gender roles – instead of making his wife work in the garden while he lazily smokes a pipe, he happily harvests the vegetables and brings them to the kitchen where his wife is preparing the meal. This curious story is told without recourse to the kind of parallel editing discussed above. Instead, Guy employs a narrative style perhaps now more associated with an earlier filmmaking period. Each scene is discrete. Introduced by an inter-title that describes what we will see, the scenes depict separate incidents in a strictly chronological sequence. Some of the scenes are staged in depth and consist of a single shot reminiscent of the style we have seen employed by European filmmakers such as Yevgeni Bauer, Louis Feuillade and Gustavo Serena. The first scene depicting the wife pulling the cart is shot like this, for instance, as is the trial scene. Other scenes use continuity editing styles closer to the ones described above – the 'third lesson' where Ivan is forcing his wife to work in the garden while he relaxes is constructed using a series of shot/reverse-shots – the image of the wife toiling in the garden is shown from Ivan's point of view as he relaxes on the veranda, while the image of him relaxing approximates the wife's point of view as she looks up from her work, so that, as in Griffith's and Weber's films, the editing itself creates the space in which the drama plays out. Although *Making an American Citizen* with its eclectic mixture of shooting styles may seem anomalous compared to the Griffith and Weber films discussed above, it still adheres to the key principle of the continuity style which is to keep the audience orientated at all times, and make the story as easy to follow as possible. Guy's more generous use of inter-titles explaining the action can also be seen as part of this style. European art directors were often celebrated for their ability to dispense with inter-titles and tell the story purely in through visual means. F. W. Murnau famously employed only one title in *The Last Laugh*, and the British director Anthony Asquith employed considerable ingenuity in conveying idiomatic speech through visual means alone in films like *Shooting Stars* (1928) and *A Cottage on Dartmoor* (1929). By contrast, Hollywood filmmakers did not balk from using explanatory inter-titles in the service of narrative economy and clarity. *The Unknown* (Tod Browning, 1927) opens with precisely the sort of scene-setting inter-title which is reminiscent of Alice Guy's practice, and which continued to be used into the sound period: 'This is a story they tell in old Madrid…' The heroine of the film, Nanon (Joan Crawford), has a phobia of men's hands – a central narrative theme which you might think would take quite some time to convey in a silent film. We see her shrink from the embrace of the circus strong man (Norman Kerry), although confusingly she also seems to be attracted to him. Browning wastes no time in making the explanation explicit through an inter-title: 'Hands! Men's hands! How I hate them!', she says to herself, while wringing her own and displaying them to the camera. Later on in the film, the absolute clarity established through recourse to such explicit storytelling techniques pays off in a brilliant *coup de théâtre*, which requires no explanatory inter-title at all. The strongman's rival for Nanon, Alonzo (Lon Chaney), knowing of her phobia, seizes on the idea of cutting off his own arms in order to win her. A chance remark from his companion, followed by a close-up of Alonzo's face as the idea dawns on him, and the horrified reaction of his friend, is enough to convey this development, without the need to explain what is being said.

Women, Immigrants, Stars

Lois Weber and Alice Guy were not the only women working in key filmmaking roles in the American industry at this time. Jane Gaines lists almost twenty production companies controlled or owned by women in the early silent period, reiterating Anthony Slide's observation that there were more women directors working in the American industry before 1920 than at any subsequent period in its history. As Gaines comments, 'The existence of so many companies points, if nothing else, to the numerical importance of women at this stage and yet this knowledge has yet to have an influence on the film history we have been teaching (2002: 90). The contributions of such women, not only as directors and producers, but also in technical roles such as camera operators, colourists and editors can now be more easily assessed thanks to the work of Gaines and others on the 'Women Film Pioneers Project' online resource, which collects together scholarship, biographies and resources about the many women working in the film industry during the silent period.[1] One possible explanation for the wealth of women working in key roles in this period, compared to the rather more impoverished opportunities open to them in later years might be to do with the relatively fluid nature of many working practices before the mid-1920s. As roles became more strictly defined in later years, so particular jobs became gendered, and women were pushed out of activities such as directing into other departments, some of which continued to be associated with powerful and influential female industry figures – scriptwriting and editing, for example. Although Alice Guy left the industry around 1920, Lois Weber continued to make feature films into the sound period. Other female producers included Mary Pickford and Alla Nazimova, while writers such as June Mathis and Elinor Glynn wielded considerable power in the studios.

Returning briefly to *Making an American Citizen* we might also note that, like *The Unseen Enemy* and *Suspense*, it is typical of American cinema in the efficiency with which it stitches its narrative to an ideological argument about American culture. Modern audiences may recognise the way in which the immigrants' native culture is vilified and held up to ridicule as brutal, backward and uncivilised. This is offered not so much as a true representation of peasant culture in Imperial Russia, but as a foil against which to contrast American culture as modern, civilised and humane. Ivan's transformation into a civilised husband is coterminous with his assimilation as an 'American citizen'. The immigrant experience is often invoked in histories of early cinema, perhaps because cinema's development coincided with a period of the greatest influx of European immigrants from the 1890s through to 1924. The nickelodeons of Manhattan are portrayed as particularly popular with immigrant communities – a forging ground for new identities, but also for the developing film industry itself. Hollywood moguls such as William Fox (of Twentieth Century Fox), Adolph Zukor (of Paramount) and Marcus Loew (of MGM) were immigrants or the sons of immigrants, and started their careers as entrepreneurs running nickelodeons in New York (see Singer 2003: 129). Lucy Fischer notes that an increasing backlash against immigration occurred in the popular culture of the mid-1920s, and vexed questions of ethnicity, exoticism and 'Americanness' informed the discourse around many extremely popular stars of the late 1910s and early 1920s, notably Rudolph Valentino, who was Italian in origin but played characters with a variety of 'exotic' ethnicities, and Sessue Hayakawa whose films such as *The Cheat* (Cecil B. DeMille, 1915) and *The Secret Game* (William C. DeMille, 1917) are remarkable in the way they oscillate between erotic fascination with, and hysteria over, his Japanese-American identity (see Fischer 2009: 12).

Another immigrant filmmaker was Charlie Chaplin, who had been born in London in 1889 and had first arrived in America as part of a touring music hall troupe in 1911. He started making films in 1913 and by the time he directed and starred in *The Immigrant* (1917), he was easily the biggest film star, and arguably the most highly paid individual, in the world. The phenomenon of the film 'star' – a named player whose appeal was central to the publicity surrounding a film and who sold not only the films he or she appeared in, but also a range of ancillary products from photographs and magazines to cosmetics and fashion – had developed around 1909 and was already well established. But Chaplin's fame was of a different magnitude. In an age before television or the internet, he was a globally recognised icon, his image as 'the little tramp' reproduced on postcards, in magazines and newspapers, on song-sheets and in cartoons. Charles

J. Maland cites an article from 1915 that christened the craze for the star in that year 'Chaplinitis'. As Maland observes, the many profiles of the actor in newspapers and fan magazines that year emphasised his immigrant status and framed his story as the epitome of the American myth of opportunity and success. They played up the idea that Chaplin had arrived as 'a penniless immigrant stranded in New York' but that thanks to America's meritocratic culture he had been able rise, by raw talent and sheer hard work, to the pinnacle of his profession (2003: 203). Chaplin's film version of the immigrant experience is more ambivalent, although it does ultimately endorse the idea of America as a land of opportunity. As in *Making an American Citizen*, much of the humour of Chaplin's film revolves around the immigrant's failure to understand American society, and his struggle to learn the social codes necessary for survival. When they first see the Statue of Liberty from their boat, all the immigrants gather joyfully to watch it pass with hopeful and sentimental expressions on their faces. But immediately they are roped into a corner of the deck – physically restrained, ready for bureaucratic processing by the immigration officers. This contrast between expectation and reality is a gag that is repeated throughout the film. Finding himself hungry and broke in the city, the Tramp finds a coin on the pavement and, rejoicing in his luck, goes into a restaurant to spend it. He has not noticed that the coin has immediately fallen through a hole in his pocket, and back to the place where he found it. The waiter of the restaurant rather aggressively educates him in American table manners, making him remove his hat. Other misapprehensions about the correct use of cutlery are also a source of humour. Observing the punishment that is meted out to those who can't pay, the Tramp discovers the loss of his coin and anticipates the paying of his bill with great apprehension. He tries various ruses that don't pay off, but eventually through his ingenuity and enterprise, he engineers a solution.

In many ways, perhaps, the film star is the axiomatic symbol of American cinema in the 1920s. Stars existed in other popular cinemas as we have seen, but it was Hollywood that really developed the star into a quintessentially cinematic phenomenon. Indeed, the readiness with which Hollywood attracted stars such as Pola Negri and Greta Garbo from Europe, reconfiguring them into even more potent lightening rods for public desire than their home industries had ever achieved for them, is a testament to this. It was not only ideas about gender and national characteristics that people took from the cinema. They were also influenced in their notions of what was stylish, what was desirable and what was erotically attainable. Alongside films a whole range of ancillary industries grew to serve these interests. Fan magazines, emerging initially as film story magazines in the 1910s, soon came to be dominated by an interest in stars and through this connection, became a primary site of self-fashioning for their readers. By consuming the magazines' stories about stars – what they wore, how they spent their leisure time, what they thought on pressing issues of the day, what their houses looked like, what their ambitions were – readers were presented with a range of possible strategies for presenting themselves to the world. Advertisements, as well as cinema publicity tie-ins and other commercial endorsements emphasised this possibility, implying that even in the use of a relatively inexpensive soap or face powder, a connection with the star was possible. Writers such as Gaylyn Studlar, Lisa Stead and Jane Bryan have emphasised the particular address of such publications to 'girls', and while cinema was popular with all kinds of audiences, there was an assumption among publishers and filmmakers in the period that the film 'fan' was specifically young and female (1999: 262).[2] Commentators at the time worried about the passivity of such 'fans', characterising them as empty-headed dreamers, sponges soaking up whatever foolish desires advertisers chose to plant in their fertile minds. By contrast, modern scholars are more likely to interpret fan-cultures as active forums for self-fashioning – sites of contradictory discourses which could promote criticism of and resistance to cultural expectations as much as conformity.

In the early 1920s a series of scandals involving the Hollywood community generated national coverage and offered a warning to the studios about the dangers of negative publicity. The film director William Desmond Taylor was found murdered in his home in Los Angeles in 1922, and the frenzied press speculation which followed cited various well-known stars as possible suspects (see Higham 2004). The matinée idol Wallace Reid died of morphine addiction in 1923 having initially been prescribed the drug by the studios themselves in an attempt to keep him working (although this fact was suppressed at the time) (see Korszarski 1994: 278). Most notoriously, the comedian Roscoe 'Fatty' Arbuckle was accused of the rape and murder of a starlet at a drunken party in 1921. After three trials Arbuckle was finally acquitted in 1922, but his career never recovered, partly because the studios, keen to distance themselves from such scandals, refused to employ him. It was against the background of such scandals and considerable criticism of the industry on moral grounds, that the Motion Picture Producers and Distributors of America (MPPDA) was formed. This lobbying organisation, under the directorship of Will Hays, operated in the interests of all of the studios, representing the industry in financial and government circles but also importantly laying down recommendations for the moral conduct of stars, and the clean content of films. The MPPDA's advice was only in the form of loose guidance. Actual film censorship was a matter for local authorities and differed from place to place. The more stringent censorship of the Production Code did not occur until the 1930s, so films from the 1920s often seem surprisingly risqué to modern audiences.

Flappers and It

If studios and fan magazines assumed that young women were their most important market, the 'flapper' was the most visible and discussed version of young womanhood in the 1920s. Emblematic of the changes occurring in gender roles, but also of shifts in work and leisure practices, attitudes to sex and (particularly female) sexuality, the term originated at the turn of the century. By the 1920s it had come to refer to young women who had left school but who had not yet married and who enjoyed a degree of freedom and independence denied to previous generations of women. The 'flapper' had the vote, the freedom to pursue a career and the liberty and the disposable income to enjoy the new consumer culture. A symbol of American modernity, she took full advantage of the opportunities consumerism offered for self-fashioning, for leisure and for the pursuit of pleasure. 'Flapper' fashions, which started at the foundation garments – abandoning the corset in favour of 'step-ins' – and extended to short skirts, bobbed hair, stockings rolled down below the knee, and a taste for jazz, parties and the cinema, were merely the outward manifestations of a more fundamental shift in attitudes towards feminine roles. It was the interest in pleasure, and particularly sexual freedom that made the flapper an object of obsessive fascination to magazine and newspaper columnists and moral commentators across the nation. As Studlar observes, the spectre of the flapper was viewed as an almost apocalyptic threat to traditional American morals, and her attitude to sex was seen to be 'usurping a male prerogative more powerful and precious than the vote… Universal suffrage and female employment were not cited as the chief culprits in these distressing trends; women's assertion of their right to seek sexual gratification was' (1999: 276).

Of course, the flapper was also good for business. Articles about her controversial habits sold newspapers, songs detailing her charms and her vices topped the music charts, and numerous popular Broadway shows such as Jerome Kern's *Sunny* (1925) and Vincent Youman's *No, No, Nanette* (1925) celebrated her adventures. In the title song of the latter show ('No, no, Nanette! That's all I hear!), the flapper heroine quotes the reaction of her elders whenever she expresses her desire to have fun, whether that be by driving cars, smoking cigarettes, or more louche activities. She publicly declares her intention to go off the leash for a little while. The show's hit song, 'Tea for Two', is sung to Nanette by her fiancé and paints an idyllic picture of their future life as a couple ('Just me for you and you for me'), but in her responding verse, Nanette rejects this future, telling him that she'd 'rather wait, dear, for some future date, dear', because in the meantime she plans to have some fun. Nevertheless romantic love ultimately triumphs over hedonism, and at the end of the show the couple are reunited to the sound of wedding bells. This same ambivalence – a celebration of the sexual agency of the flapper, ultimately contained by the triumph of romantic love and marriage – also marks the numerous films which showcased her as a figure and were marketed to young female cinema fans who aspired to her status. Studlar stresses that the conservative closure of such films might not in fact close down the radical potential they offered to female cinemagoers, citing evidence from fan magazines and sociologists which suggests that 'the narrative closure regulating female sexuality was not necessarily what young women remembered of the films' (1999: 281). She also points out that the films remain vague about how marriage might alter their heroines' future behaviour. Either way, many such films were produced throughout the decade, repeatedly showcasing stars such as Bebe Daniels, Marion Davis, Colleen Moore, Joan Crawford and Clara Bow. In several of these films, the cinema itself appears as a key reference point for the flapper heroine. In *Ella Cinders* (Alfred E. Green, 1926), Ella (Colleen Moore) enters a competition to become a film star – a long shot which she acknowledges as her only hope of escaping from her small town and the tyranny of her Cinderella-like life skivvying for her mother and two stepsisters. Unexpectedly she wins, not because of her beauty but because of her comedic appearance, but on arriving in Hollywood she discovers that the competition had been a fraud. Alone and friendless, she must use her own ingenuity to blag her way into the studio and through a series of fortuitous accidents lands a contract, and returns to her home town and her sweetheart, a star. In *The Patsy* (King Vidor, 1928), Patricia (Marion Davis) is also under the thumb of a tyrannical mother and sister. But as an avid film fan, she attempts to model herself on the personalities in the movies. In one particularly entertaining sequence she tries to get out of a scrape by imitating a variety of popular stars (embodying different feminine 'types'), including Pola Negri, Mae Murray and Lillian Gish.

Perhaps the most famous flapper film is *It*, starring Clara Bow. Bow was the quintessential flapper figure, appearing as such in numerous films over a short but prolific career. Her staggering output (she averaged over twelve films a year in the mid- to late 1920s) is a testament to perfection with which she embodied the zeitgeist of the period. An implicit connection between Bow herself and the film fans who viewed her was written into her star image – born of working-class origins and a film fan herself, she became a star partly as a result of entering the 'fame and fortune' acting contest run by *Brewster's Magazine* in 1921. *It* does not explicitly refer to cinema in the way that the films mentioned above do. But it is extremely self-reflexive about the special quality that distinguishes its own star. The opening title card offers a definition of that quality which lends the film its title, a definition made famous (and signed) by the writer, Elinor Glyn:

> 'IT' is that quality possessed by some which draws all others with its magnetic force. With 'IT' you win all men if you are a woman – and all women if you are a man. 'IT' can be a quality of the mind as well as a physical attraction.

We are next introduced to Cyrus Waltham (Antonio Moreno), the good-looking heir to Waltham's department store and his somewhat foppish friend Monty (William Austin). Monty is reading the latest issue of *Cosmopolitan*, in which appeared the article by Elinor Glyn about 'it' on which the film itself is based. Having absorbed a further definition of 'it' by Glyn, he looks at his own face in the mirror, trying to detect the quality in himself. Monty's evaluative gaze establishes the motif of the

Fig. 12: *It* (1927);
the power of the gaze –
Betty Lou (Clara Bow)
eyes up her boss.

film, which, as Marsha Orgeron has pointed out, is very much built upon the exchange of desiring 'looks' (2003: 84). When the men go on to the shop-floor it is Waltham who becomes the object of desirous looks – a gaggle of female shop assistants are shown gazing at him appreciatively from behind their counter, with Betty Lou (Clara Bow) in the foreground. 'Sweet Santa Claus,' she exclaims in an inter-title, 'give me *him*.' This desiring feminine gaze absolutely reverses the usual pattern observed in later Hollywood filmmaking by feminist theorists such as Laura Mulvey, who suggest that, usually, looking and desiring is the prerogative of the male protagonist.

For Betty Lou though, the difficulty is to get Waltham to look at her at all. He fails to return her gaze, even when she drops her purse at his feet. Monty, by contrast, is intent on inspecting all of the shop girls to see if they have 'it'. He walks along the counter looking at each one individually to no avail. A memorable sequence shows us a close-up of him looking around the shop, his head turning slowly through 180 degrees until he catches sight of Betty Lou gazing lustfully at Waltham, standing just beside him. We see Monty's point of view – a close-up of Betty Lou. Then we see *her* point of view – a close-up of Waltham, the object of her desiring gaze. Then we return to the shot of Betty looking, before returning to her point of view in a slightly wider shot which shows both Monty and Waltham – Waltham obliviously chatting to another executive, while Monty, looking directly back at Betty, realises that he's found a girl with 'it'. Through continuity editing, and the exchange of glances, the sequence eloquently establishes the relationship of desire between the three characters. When Monty invites Betty to dinner, she insists that he take her to the Ritz, where she knows Waltham will be. In a sequence which seems to predict Kracauer's comment in 'The Little Shopgirls go to the Movies' that, rather than ordinary girls dreaming of marrying the owners of Rolls Royces, it is the owners of Rolls Royces that dream that ordinary girls fantasise about them, Betty won't even allow Monty to drive her home in his car (1995: 292). Instead she insists that he rides on the bus with her. A later sequence makes clear the difference between the modernity of Betty Lou's flapper sensibility and a more traditional femininity. Betty's preparations for the Ritz are intercut with those of Adela Van Doren, Waltham's elegant fiancée. The stately Adela is shown gazing in the mirror at a massive dressing table, while a maid primps her hair and lays out her new dress. Meanwhile, Betty Lou recruits her flatmate to help her cut the sleeves off her work dress with the kitchen scissors in order to transform it into an evening gown. She improvises a corsage by pulling the trim from an old hat. The hat is wrapped in a newspaper featuring an advertisement for Waltham's department store and Betty pauses to contemplate its announcement of the 'Charming new dresses' sold at Walthams, and the 'latest fashions from Paris'. As Orgeron points out, this moment underlines the idea that Betty Lou's desire is

> double: it is at once for Waltham and also for what he represents in consumer culture. Further, Bow's desire for Waltham and his gaze is integral to her longing to be recognised by and within consuming culture, for as a working girl it seems that only a man like Waltham (interchangeable as his name is with the department store) can legitimate her consuming desires. (2003: 90)

Once at the restaurant, Betty Lou's 'consuming desires' are again expressed through a series of 'looks' conveyed primarily through editing. She is looked up and down and judged by the waiter, who suggests an out-of-the-way table to Monty. But Betty is not to be outmanoeuvred so easily. She demands to be seated in the centre of the restaurant. In a sequence which matches the earlier one of Monty surveying the department store, we see her slowly gaze around the restaurant, turning her head slowly through

360 degrees. Her gaze finally latches onto Waltham, and the camerawork literalises her desire, transforming her point of view shot into a dramatic dolly-in, making Waltham appear to zoom from a long-shot to a close-up – the centre of Betty Lou's attention and desire. Here, finally, Waltham is induced to return her gaze and acknowledge that she, like him, possesses 'it'. Later in the meal, while pulling a wish-bone with Monty, she gazes straight at Waltham and says 'I'm going to get my wish', and the audience is left in no doubt about how the film will end.

Like other flapper films, then, *It* is remarkable for its celebration of female desire and sexual agency, and this can even be read through the editing style of the film, as we have seen. Such freedoms are not offered without warning though. Betty Lou has to work hard to negotiate a relationship on her own terms. Waltham initially offers her a 'left handed arrangement' – apparently content to set her up as his mistress. Betty holds out for marriage, and braves the social contempt of Waltham's set in order to get it. Her ability to overcome the class divide, as well as the rewards she reaps for her determined pursuit of her heart's desire, feed into some of the fundamental myths of American culture of the period.

I have emphasised the ways in which Hollywood addressed young female audiences through the 'flapper' films here, but as Bordwell points out, the sheer volume of Hollywood's output in this period is overwhelming. Part of the industry's success (as we have seen) is in the consistency of its products – their standardisation in terms of a certain level of polish, but also in terms of a reliable set of conventions to do with aspects such as editing, lighting and (most importantly) storytelling. But another factor in the industry's success is in the variety of its output and its appeal to different audiences through genre. The 'flapper' films offer a distinct mixture of feminine appeal, fashion and light-hearted romance. Other genres emerged emphasising exoticism, heroism, patriotism and prestige. Westerns, war films, melodramas and historical epics offered a variety of pleasures to international audiences across the board – but always with stories and stars at the centre.

Notes

1   The Women Film Pioneers Project is available at https://wfpp.cdrs. columbia.edu/about/

2 See also: J. Bryan (2006) '"The cinema looking glass": The British film fan magazine, 1911–1918' (unpublished PhD thesis), University of East Anglia. L. Stead (forthcoming) 'Dear Cinema Girls: Girlhood, Picturegoing and the Interwar Film Magazine', in C. Clay, M. DiCenzo, B. Green, F. Hackney (eds) *Women's Periodicals and Print Culture in Britain, 1918–1939: The Interwar Period*. Edinburgh: Edinburgh University Press.

5   BRITAIN – LOOKING TWO WAYS

The British producer in considering technique would do well to look, like Janus, in two ways – to California certainly, but to Berlin as well. He may look two ways and move in neither, remaining British.

– Iris Barry (The Bioscope, 1924)

I am persuaded that what the average intelligent cinema-goer likes is something halfway between the Caligari stuff, in which people look like parallelograms and furniture in rhomboid, and the nit-wit film in which stenographers renounce diamonds and protection for the horny-handed wistfulness of some virginal cow-puncher. Most cinema-goers, I am persuaded, just want a reasonably good story, reasonably well told.

– James Agate (The Tatler, 1930)

Some readers may be surprised to find a chapter devoted to British cinema here. Unlike the cinemas of America, Germany and Russia, the British cinema of the 1920s isn't associated with any particular international brand or aesthetic of filmmaking. It was certainly not admired by serious film critics and intellectuals, either at the time or later. Indeed, quite the opposite was the case. British cinema was actively despised by many of those whose writing was instrumental in establishing the importance of

German expressionist and Soviet montage cinema and in recognising the skill and talent behind the commercial strength of American cinema. Paul Rotha, in his 1930 survey of *The Film Till Now*, argued that 'the British film has never been self-sufficient in that it has never achieved its independence' (1967: 381). For him, the British film lacked 'honest conception', British studios were 'filled with persons of third rate intelligence' who displayed a 'feeble mentality' and by 1930 were still 'just beginning to grasp the rudimentary principles of film construction'; as a result, he declared:

> Analysis of the output of British studios since the war is impossible in the same way as has been done with that of other countries… I am unable to discern a realistic, expressionistic, naturalistic, decorative, or any other phase in the development of the British cinema. Added to which there are no tendencies to be traced, for British films do not have tendencies… (Ibid.)

Rotha's book did not go wholly unchallenged at the time (the Agate quotation above comes from his review of *The Film Till Now*), but the book remained in print, in revised and updated versions, until the late 1960s and was many scholars' introduction to film criticism. His position, moreover, reflected the attitude of the most influential journal of 'serious' film criticism of the 1920s, *Close Up*, which also tended to sneer at British cinema, when it chose to acknowledge it at all.

In the face of this damning assessment, it is perhaps not surprising that later generations of critics did not feel inclined to open the archives and re-visit the British films of the period for themselves. The judgement of Rotha went unchallenged, and was echoed in all of the standard works on British cinema almost to the end of the twentieth century, while the vast majority of the films themselves languished unseen in the archives. Perhaps the only exception to this rule was the early work of Alfred Hitchcock, particularly *The Lodger* (1926) and *Blackmail* (1929). But familiarity with these films didn't lead to curiosity about the output of others, since Hitchcock himself (especially in later life) liked to convey the impression that he had been a lone genius in Britain, working alongside a collection of amateurs. As late as 1999 it was still possible to pronounce on the British cinema of the 1920s without apparently having seen any of the films.

Why, then, include a chapter on British cinema here? Firstly, because the recent revival of interest in British film of this period, the discovery of many excellent but hitherto unknown films, the work of contextualising them and reconstructing the careers of their producers and histories of their production companies, offers an object lesson in the benefits to be gained from questioning, and looking beyond the established canon. Just as there is more to 1920s German and Russian cinema than expressionism and montage, this revisionist work has revealed that there is more to British cinema than the void indicated by Rotha. Secondly, the history of British cinema in the 1920s offers a parallel and a contrast to the histories of the German and Russian cinemas. We have seen how Germany and Russia, due to different circumstances, were initially sheltered from the necessity of competing with Hollywood and how each industry developed a particular 'style' which circulated internationally. We have seen how each industry also strove to maintain a popular cinematic output, and sought later in the decade through a variety of mechanisms to manage the potential competition between domestic productions and those imported from America.

British filmmakers faced similar challenges with regard to the difficulty of competing with an extremely strong Hollywood export industry. Without the 'protection' of hyper-inflation or of war trade sanctions, the British exhibition market felt the full force of American export energies. The popularity of US films with British audiences had been well established throughout the war period and by the 1920s over 80% of films shown in British cinemas came from Hollywood. This was good news for cinema owners and distributors, but bad news for film producers, who struggled both to find finance for their productions, and to find space in the cinemas to show them once they were made. It created anxiety in government circles too. Culturally and industrially, a strong domestic film production industry was understood to be important for the health of the nation. As Sir Philip Cunliffe Lister told parliament in 1927, 'the cinema is today the most universal means through which national ideas and national atmosphere can be spread' (Anon. 1927: 2039); films were shown throughout the Empire, he said, and through those films the peoples of the Empire formed their 'ideas and outlook' (ibid.). Films were thought to have an economic impact too, not just through box office returns, but through the principle that 'trade follows the film' – that the display of consumer goods on the screen stimulated demand for those products in the audience, which had a knock-on effect on domestic manufacturing industries. These arguments were being made in British film circles throughout the decade, but it wasn't until a perceived crisis in the industry around 1924, when some key producers went bankrupt, that the government started seriously to consider protective legislation similar to the 'contingency' acts in Germany. The Cinematograph Act, which was passed in 1927, achieved limited success in guaranteeing British films space in British cinemas and in encouraging the development of several properly capitalised vertically integrated film companies toward the end of the decade.

Aesthetically the British industry of the 1920s was as 'Janus-faced' as Iris Barry suggested that it should be (1924: 29). Before 1924, British producers might be understood to have 'looked to Berlin' – not in the sense of imitating the aesthetics of expressionism, but rather in attempting to develop their own distinctive visual and storytelling style and to market it as an alternative to the dominant mode of Hollywood filmmaking – a form of product differentiation which might create British film as a recognisable 'brand'. Later in the decade, filmmakers drew more heavily on Hollywood models, heeding calls for a faster narrative and editing pace, and better stars. At the same time (Janus-like) they drew inspiration from developments in European cinema, incorporating elements of expressionism and montage techniques, but also through the 'Film Europe' movement, establishing transnational working practices and filmmaking alliances. Hitchcock's famous sojourn in Berlin was just one of many such exchanges.

Cecil Hepworth and the Pictorialist Tradition

British filmmakers hadn't always been thought inept. Some of the key pioneers of the 1890s had been British, including Cecil Hepworth, whose *How it Feels to Be Run Over* and *Explosion of a Motor Car* (both 1900) are still celebrated as exemplars of the innovative way in which early filmmakers explored qualities unique to cinema such as trick photography, at the same time as playfully processing contemporary concerns about technology and modernity. Hepworth's background was as a commercial photographer and magic lantern showman, and some of his early films, such as *Alice in Wonderland* (1903) have the feel and structure of a magic lantern show. By contrast, his company's famous

Rescued by Rover (Lewin Fitzhamon, 1905) is often held up as a major advance in the kind of continuity editing techniques that would later be developed to perfection by figures like D. W. Griffith in America. As the dog Rover rushes from his master's home to the squalid slum where the tramp who kidnapped the family child is hiding, and then back to alert his master of the child's whereabouts, and back again accompanied by his master to rescue the child, the camera cuts fluently between the various stages of his journey, describing the space and the action with what Charles Barr has called 'a machine-like efficiency ... a structural principle of repetition and variation, of permutations worked upon a limited number of camera set-ups' (2003: 14) which predicted not only the technique adopted by Griffith, but the whole of the American continuity system. Barr expresses surprise that having made such a breakthrough, Hepworth appears to have turned his back on this sort of filmmaking and returned to the tableaux style exemplified by *Alice in Wonderland*: 'It's as if he and [other British pioneers] ran the first lap, passed on the baton to the Americans and then stopped exhausted' (ibid.).

Hepworth wasn't exhausted though, as Barr himself admits. He changed his filmmaking style, but continued to make films for another twenty years, running one of the most successful and significant British companies of the 1910s and early 1920s. In many ways he continued to innovate, establishing an 'in house' fan magazine, *The Hepworth Picture Play Paper*, in 1915 and fostering a roster of regular players who he meticulously built up as stars, particularly Alma Taylor who was voted the top star of 1915 and for some audiences attained the status of 'our English Mary Pickford' (Burrows 2001: 30). The Hepworth company produced a broad range of films throughout the 1910s, including travelogues, comic burlesques as well as public information films devised for the Ministry of Information during the war, for instance *Broken in the Wars* (Cecil Hepworth, 1918). The company also successfully made long-running comic series, such as those starring Alma Taylor and Chrissie White as the 'Tilly sisters' – a series that began with *Tilly the Tomboy Visits the Poor* (Lewin Fitzhamon, 1910) and ran intermittently until 1915. A later series starred John Butt as 'Tubby', for instance in *Tubby's Rest Cure* (Frank Wilson, 1916). From the late 1910s and through the early 1920s, though, the company began specialising in a particular kind of melodramatic feature film. Often these were adapted from well-known plays or novels of the period, such as *Trelawny of the Wells* (Cecil Hepworth, 1916) from the stage play by Arthur Wing Pinero, and *Alwyn* (Henry Edwards, 1920) from the smash-hit bestselling novel by Theodore Watts-Dutton. Sometimes they even offered stories inspired by (and quoting) popular artworks – such as *Pipes of Pan* (Cecil Hepworth, 1923), inspired by *The Piper of Dreams* by Estella Canziani. What these films had in common, apart from their intertextual references to theatre, novels and paintings, was an emphasis on pictorialism – on the film image as a pictorial composition carefully arranged and beautifully photographed to bring out its innately aesthetic qualities as much as its narrative function.

Andrew Higson links Hepworth's pictorialism with earlier traditions of 'artistic photography' (1995: 51). Christine Gledhill emphasises the tendency of many British filmmakers of the early 1920s towards 'picture making' – a practice that reaches back to nineteenth-century traditions of theatrical and artistic storytelling embedded within a wider culture of visual narration (2003: 31). Both scholars understand this emphasis on the pictorial as a conscious decision by the filmmaker – an attempt to create a national style of filmmaking distinct from that of Hollywood – rather than evidence of their 'failure' to understand the 'rudimentary principles of film construction'. Higson describes these aesthetics as part of a strategy of 'product differentiation', arguing that,

> to accuse such films of being primitive, or uncinematic, or too literary, or too theatrical, as many critics have done over the years, is to fail to take into account the particular conditions of this differentiation. Uncinematic may simply mean not like classical Hollywood cinema – but, as this is typically one of the objectives of the heritage film, it is hardly a valid criticism. (1995: 28)

For Higson, Hepworth's films such as *Comin thro' the Rye* (1924) can be understood as precursors to the 'heritage' genre that became particularly associated with British cinema from the 1980s onwards – films with pretensions to 'art house' status, which relied on similar compositional standards, showcasing country houses, period costumes and striking rural landscapes in the leisurely retelling of a known literary classic. His argument is primarily reliant on a reading of *Comin' thro the Rye*, Hepworth's final film, and the only one that was available to view at the time he was writing. Although most of Hepworth's films from this period do not survive, some further examples have come to light since Higson's account, which suggest perhaps a more concentrated concern with showcasing a variety of English rural landscapes. They revolve around the hardships experienced particularly by women in rural communities which are marked by a strongly patriarchal power structure, rather than dealing with the country house aesthetics associated with more recent heritage films. *Helen of Four Gates* (1920), *Tansy* (1921), *Pipes of Pan* (1923) and *Mist in the Valley* (1923) all showcase different areas of the British rural landscape, and all star Alma Taylor as young heroines more or less adrift in their social milleaux.

In *Helen of Four Gates*, Helen (Taylor) is an orphan who is raised on a remote Yorkshire farm by the malevolent Abel Mason (James Carew). Mason had been her mother's lover, but he was jilted in favour of her father when the hereditary insanity in his family was revealed. Obsessively, Mason harbours this grudge, bringing Helen up to believe herself his daughter and that insanity will be her own inheritance. He drives away her lover and forces her to marry his old friend Fielding Day (John MacAndrews), knowing that at his hand she will be brutalised. As he says when proposing the match to Day, 'Marry yon lass, wed her, mak her as miserable as only a hellspawn like thee can mak a woman…'. Other dialogue titles also reproduce the Yorkshire dialect of the novel, and the film is shot on location around Hebden Bridge, making full use of the extraordinary beauty of the hill country landscape (*Tansy* offers a similar showcasing of the very different Sussex landscape). Hepworth frames his scenes according to pictorialist principles. Characters are often positioned on the hillside to one side of the frame, while the valley falls away behind them, drawing the eye across the expanse of landscape that occupies the majority of the image. In some cases, scenes are staged in depth using a blocking technique reminiscent of the style employed ten years earlier by Yevgeni Bauer and Gustavo Serena, as already discussed. Despite his reputation for making slow-moving films, though, Hepworth never holds the shot for as long as those filmmakers do. After an altercation with Mason, Helen's lover Martin (George Dewhurst) declares he will stand by her whatever might happen. We see the couple comforting each other, sitting on a wall above the picturesque stone farmhouse. The front door of the house is visible in the background, behind and some way below them. Out of this door, Mason emerges. He slowly approaches them carrying a missive,

Fig. 13: *Helen of Four Gates* (1920); landscape and deep staging – Helen (Alma Taylor) awaits her lover, but he avoids her by cutting across the hillside.

which he tells Martin to deliver to an insane relative. His intention is that Martin should witness the insanity in the family at first hand and thus be encouraged to break his promise to Helen. Having made his request, he retreats again to the background of the image, pausing to glance behind – checking the lovers' reaction before re-entering the house. A later scene shows a rhyming composition. Helen is waiting in the lane for Martin to return. Behind her the lane stretches away into the landscape, but while she is gazing forward we see her lover approach in the far background. He notices her waiting for him, and cuts off across the hillside in order to avoid her. Mason's scheme has worked.

Unusually for a filmmaker working as late as 1920, Hepworth very rarely cuts into a scene – there are few close-ups or point of view shots and no shot/reverse-shot structures. Hepworth's carefully composed framings are often held for the duration of the scene, with editing kept to a minimum. Indeed, edits are almost never straight cuts, but always fade swiftly to black and then fade up again – a system which has left Hepworth open to charges of incompetence, and of clinging to filming techniques long after they had become outdated and old-fashioned. Nevertheless, the films were often well received, and when Hepworth went bankrupt in 1924, it was arguably as a result of ambitious over-expansion in the wake of the financial success of his *Alf's Button* (1920), rather than because his films had no domestic market. Hepworth's editing style is perhaps a particularly controversial idiosyncrasy, but he was not alone among British filmmakers of the early 1920s in absolutely striving to showcase the English rural landscape in stories that drew on both canonised and popular literary works, and dramatised the tensions between the town and the country, modernity and the past. Such characteristics today evoke associations with nostalgic and perhaps reactionary visions of England's rural past as an ideal and unchanging fantasy space, and these are often the charges leveled against the films by critics who have never seen them. They are hard to sustain in the face of the brutal and dystopian portrayal of rural life offered in films such as *Tansy* and *Helen of Four Gates*. Indeed one might read the latter's theme as precisely about the futility of attempting to shackle the present generation to the sins and attitudes of the past. At the end of the film, of course, Abel Mason is defeated, and Helen is free to marry her lover.

The cycle of romances starring the popular couple Guy Newell and Ivy Duke and made for George Clarke productions also showcased rural landscapes in stories that dramatised the relationship between the country and the city, and celebrated the modernising tendency of the interaction of those two worlds. In *The Lure of Crooning Water* (Arthur Rooke, 1920) Duke plays a burnt-out actress who takes a rest-cure on Newell's farm and embarks on a quite startlingly erotic affair with him. Its sister film, *The Garden of Resurrection* (Arthur Rooke, 1920) reverses the situation, with Newell as a dandy who has lost his taste for life, and is only diverted from his suicidal thoughts when he meets Duke during a holiday in the spectacular landscape of the Cornish coast. Gledhill suggests that such pastoral settings might be understood to be sites of 'transformation'. 'Landscape in films', she suggests, 'provides story space in which encounters between travelling and located protagonists take place, leading to re-evaluations and negotiations between urban modernity and relinquished pastoral ideals' (2007: 38).

A final set of films which, while not technically showcasing rural settings, nevertheless placed great emphasis on location shooting and picturesque British scenery, are the nautical comedies based on W. W. Jacobs' stories, scripted by Lydia Hayward and directed by Manning Haynes for Artistic. These were completely forgotten until they were brought out of the archive as part of the British Silent Film Festival run by Bryony Dixon and Laraine Porter (an event which since its inception in 1998, has been largely responsible for the extensive re-appraisal of British silent cinema).

Films such as *Sam's Boy* (1922), *The Skipper's Wooing* (1922) and *The Boatswain's Mate* (1924) found great popularity with contemporary festival audiences, who saw in them a distinctively British style of filmmaking, coupled with the strong story lines and well-paced editing to compete with the best of American cinema. The films are primarily light comedies set in the coastal shipping communities around the Thames Estuary and the Medway. In *Sam's Boy* an orphan boy 'adopts' Sam, the skipper of a small ship, pretending he is his father in order to hitch a cruise from London up to Kent. He will brook no opposition, but when he insists on following Sam home, Sam's wife has a thing or two to say about the situation. *The Skipper's Wooing* also offers a gentle travelogue as the rivals for the heroine's hand tour the coast in an attempt to find her father who has absconded under the mistaken impression that he is responsible for a shipmate's death. In one elegant sequence, the father – who is illiterate – mistakes the 'missing person' notices posted by his daughter for posters declaring him 'wanted for murder'. As he gazes at the poster featuring his image, the English writing accompanying it dissolves into Greek lettering, visually rendering the phrase 'it's all Greek to me', an English idiom indicating incomprehension. As well as offering picturesque portrayals of British coastal fishing villages and shipping, the films can be read as gently feminist. Gledhill (2015) argues that this – and the success of the films generally – can be largely attributed to Lydia Hayward's contribution as the adapter, scenario and inter-title writer. Hayward was one of a number of women working in the industry at the time, particularly as scenario editors and script-writers. The example of the 'wanted' poster above is typical of her crisp and witty style of storytelling. Another example can be seen in *The Boatswain's Mate*, which centres around Mrs. Walters (Florence Turner), the widowed but independent-minded landlady of a remote pub. Her regular customer George (Johnny Butt) is sweet on her. He continuously but unsuccessfully tries to persuade her to remarry, arguing that she needs a man by her side to assist her should the pub be attacked by robbers. He hits on the idea of staging a fake 'robbery' from which he can 'rescue' her, hoping that in her gratitude she will marry him. The unlikeliness of this plan's success is firmly established in a shot showing Mrs. Walters settling down for the night. Unlike the heroines in *Suspense* or *The Lonely Villa* (D. W. Griffith, 1909) she is not cowering in anxiety and fear at the loneliness and vulnerability of her situation. Instead, she is sitting comfortably in bed with a shotgun beside her, gleefully reading *Dracula* by Bram Stoker. *The Boatswain's Mate* had earlier been adapted into a one-act opera by the feminist composer Dame Ethel Smyth, and was staged at the Royal Opera House several times during the 1920s, but it is unclear whether the filmmakers saw it. Florence Turner herself is another example of the importance of women behind the camera in this period. She began as an early Vitagraph star in America, but came to England in 1913 where she set up her own production company with Laurence Trimble. She produced and starred in several notable British films, including *Daisy Doodad's Dial* (Laurence Trimble, 1914) and *East is East* (Henry Edwards, 1916).

A Crisis in the Industry?

The biggest British film company in the early 1920s was Stoll Picture Productions. Developing from Sir Oswald Stoll's nationwide chain of music hall theatres and cinemas, Stoll was initially a distribution and exhibition concern, with only a small interest in film production. It dramatically expanded its production activities as a direct reaction to the aggressive business strategies of American film companies, particularly the Goldwyn Corporation, which in 1919 sought to capitalise on Stoll's reliance on Goldwyn's product by withdrawing films already booked into the chain, and demanding a greatly inflated rental charge for their re-instatement. Jon Burrows argues that this was part of a wider move by a variety of American companies to establish their own distribution outlets in the UK, thus cutting out the British distributors altogether and enabling them to create a series of 'block booking' arrangements with exhibitors whereby all of their films in a given season would be booked in a single transaction (2003: 21). Stoll's response was to acquire a large studio complex at Cricklewood and to greatly expand its production programme, aiming to become completely independent of American imports in the future. The hastily devised flagship policy was to concentrate primarily on adaptations of known popular authors, initially under the supervision of Stoll's tireless 'house' director, Maurice Elvey. The 'Eminent British Authors' series adapted works from figures such as A. E. W. Mason, Edgar Wallace, H. G. Wells, Sir Arthur Conan Doyle and Ethel M. Dell, on the principle that such titles were largely pre-sold to a reading public. In some ways they continued the tradition discussed above, emphasising location and pictorialism and indeed some of the later George Clarke productions featuring Ivy Duke and Guy Newell appeared under this brand – particularly *Fox Farm* (Guy Newell, 1922), from the novel by Warwick Deeping, and *Boy Woodburn* (Guy Newell, 1922), from the novel by Alfred Ollivant. As with other British films from the period, the damning judgments about these films in the standard texts have recently been challenged by younger historians. Burrows rejects Rachel Low's claim that Stoll offered 'unsuitable stories, mechanically adapted', arguing instead that the evidence of the surviving prints suggests that 'the films display careful and imaginative attempts to find visual equivalents for the literary qualities of the source texts' (2003: 22).[1]

In their first few years, the 'Eminent British Authors' series were a notable financial success. But market forces continued to work against British films. American films remained more popular with audiences, and continued to dominate British screens. US distributors, having made their investment back at home, were able to undercut British firms by offering their bigger, more expensive films at a cheaper price than any home-grown production still needing to make back its costs could offer. Furthermore, the continued practice of 'block-booking' tied British cinemas up for months to come, meaning that independent British producers (i.e. ones who didn't own a chain of cinemas as Stoll did) often waited years before screens were available to show their films on. And so 1924 proved to be a 'crisis year': Hepworth went bankrupt and Artistic stopped producing. Famously, in November that year *Kinematograph Weekly* reported that every single British studio was 'dark'. The resulting press furore suggested that the industry was in desperate straits and without some form of intervention British films would cease to be made altogether. This event is notorious in British film history, although Burrows suggests that it was largely a publicity stunt by the industry itself, designed to draw attention to the structural inequalities inherent in the trade, and to encourage the government to start seriously considering a form of protectionist legislation. As he suggests, Stoll itself didn't suffer a slump in production in 1924 – quite the opposite – and it maintained its high level of output for the 1925 season (2003: 25). Nevertheless, Stoll did withdraw from production later in the decade, ceding the field (as Hepworth and Artistic were perceived to have done) to a new breed of more dynamic and modern production companies.

Late 1920s Productions – Hindle Wakes and Shooting Stars

By the latter half of the 1920s, the prospect of the Cinematograph Act was firmly on the cards, and even in anticipation of the legislation, production finance became easier to generate. Producers such as Herbert Wilcox, Victor Saville, John Maxwell and Michael Balcon came to the fore – men whose names would remain familiar through to the sound period and (with the exception of Maxwell) well into the 1950s. Balcon in particular is remembered as the head of Gainsborough Pictures, a modern vertically-integrated company with its own studios in Islington, and associated distribution and exhibition organisations, particularly after 1927 when it merged with the Gaumont-British combine, Balcon retaining overall control of production. Gainsborough quickly gained a reputation for successful, popular filmmaking which largely emphasised modernity, the city and the contemporary (in film style, if not always in story settings). The company is most famous today for the early films made by Hitchcock, particularly *The Lodger*, starring Ivor Novello. In fact, its commercial success was founded on Novello's stardom, particularly in *The Rat* (Graham Cutts, 1925) and its various sequels dealing with the louche demi-monde of the Parisian underworld. The film featured some startlingly innovative direction by Graham Cutts, particularly in his use of mobile camerawork and expressive lighting effects. These features were perhaps inspired by Cutts' several sojourns in Germany where as part of an 'exchange' deal that Balcon brokered with German studios for several Gainsborough directors, he had made *The Blackguard* (1925) at Ufa, and later *A Queen Was in the Parlour* (1927).

A good example of the transition between the early and late 1920s style can be seen in *Hindle Wakes* (Maurice Elvey, 1927), produced by Gaumont just prior to its merger with Gainsborough. Elvey was a figure associated with earlier periods of British film – he had been directing since 1913 and in fact had made a version of this story in 1918. He had also been the key director for Stoll in the early 1920s, responsible among other things for a series of now celebrated Sherlock Holmes adaptations. *Hindle Wakes* was adapted from Stanley Houghton's well-known stage play, written for Annie Horniman's Manchester repertory theatre in 1912. The play was famous for the realism of its portrayal of working-class Manchester life, and its themes of class and gender relations among the workers in the cotton industry of the North West. The film, too, was praised for its commitment to realism, and the national and regional specificity of its setting and tone – something demonstrably different from the films coming from America and Europe, but able to compete with them in quality and popularity (see Sargeant 2002: 48). Fanny Hawthorn (Estelle Brody), a cotton worker in Hindle, goes on holiday to Blackpool during 'wakes week'. She spends a night with Alan Jeffcote (John Stuart), whose father owns the mill where she works. They return to find that their secret tryst has been discovered by their parents. The families seek to avert a scandal by brokering a marriage between the two young people, but in the midst of their protracted negotiations, Fanny rejects the proposals, declaring that she will not be 'given away with a pound of tea' and that, although no longer a virgin, she will make her own way in life. The stage play opens on the return of the young couple from holiday, but as was typical for silent film adaptations, the film folds out the back-story, recounting the narrative chronologically from the very beginning. This enables Elvey to spend some time establishing the everyday atmosphere of life in the cotton town, showing the two different families waking up to a typical working day on 'Cotton Street' and 'Midas Avenue' respectively. On the cobbled streets of 'Cotton Street' the Hawthorns are woken up by the local 'knocker-up', a neighbour with a wooden leg whose job it is to walk the streets in the early morning, tapping at the upstairs windows of the back-to-back houses with a long stick to ensure the workers are up in time for the opening of the mill. Fanny swings her legs out of bed, beneath which are three pairs of shoes, symbolising three states of being – her bedroom slippers, her smart shoes and her workaday clogs. By contrast, Alan in 'Midas Street' has a cupboard full of shoes to select from. His father is a self-made man, who started life at the same level as Fanny's father, but worked his way up in business to the large house he now occupies. Elvey deftly indicates his humble origins by showing how he drinks his morning tea. Rather than wait for it to cool in the cup, he tips it into his saucer and sups it from that, as a factory hand would.

Elvey returns to the symbolism of the footwear. Having worked at the spinning machines all day, the mill girls all rush at the sound of the half-day whistle to exchange their clogs for their smart shoes – the shoes they will wear on their holiday. A shot showing the roomful of abandoned clogs indicates the freedom beckoning in 'wakes week'. Elvey's sequences shot

Fig. 14: *Hindle Wakes* (1927); class details visually expressed – mill owner Nathanial Jeffcote (Norman McKinnel) betrays his working class origins by drinking from his saucer.

on location in Blackpool are often praised for their vitality and modernity – the extremely mobile camera-work showing the roller coaster on the pleasure beach from the point of view of its occupants, and the hypnotic – almost abstract – shots of the seething mass of dancers, seen from the balcony of the Tower Ballroom, have the air of a 'city symphony'. By contrast, the second half of the film – dealing with Fanny's return, and the consequences of her liaison – are less visually adventurous. Primarily shot in interiors, they deal primarily with the discussions that dominate the play – extracting confessions from Fanny and Alan, dealing with Alan's fiancée and with his mother, who sees no reason why a marriage should be necessary. Here, Elvey employs the scene dissection and shot/reverse-shot structures typical of Hollywood films in the period, although the frequent presence of a circular mask more familiar from the 1910s makes these scenes appear much less modern than the earlier ones. As Amy Sargeant notes, 'the culmination of the drama is largely enacted in a long "stagey" sequence, often in mid shot, boxed in by three walls...' (2002: 56). Nevertheless, the scene is punctuated with close-ups offering emphasis and detail – a fist banging down on a table, a notebook ready to draw up the agreement. Sargeant argues that

> Elvey uses the frontal, proscenium staging of the family to considerable effect, which cannot be reduced to the 'recorded theatre' of a previous decade. The sequence is paced to culminate in a concentration on Fanny [who has] been excluded from the

discussion... Alan says that Fanny should be asked for her opinion and suddenly the camera swings round to present Fanny's point of view: 'I was just wondering where I come in', whereupon the others all look round at her. (Ibid.)

The moment is an electrifying *coup de théâtre*, not least because Fanny's point of view is so utterly revolutionary. 'I'm a woman, and I was your little fancy,' she tells Alan, 'you're a man and you were my little fancy. Don't you understand?' It constitutes a complete refutation of the sexual double standard that, while relatively well discussed in theatre of the period, was thoroughly alien to cinema. It's worth comparing the situation to that of Betty Lou in *It*. That film is constructed around our pleasure in witnessing Betty Lou's independence and vitality in her pursuit of Waltham. We applaud the fact that she rejects a 'left handed arrangement', and holds out instead for the security of social and economic status that marriage to 'the boss' represents. By contrast, in *Hindle Wakes* Fanny indulges her 'little fancy', but remains unrepentant. Even when marriage to the boss's son is offered, Fanny rejects it, preferring to retain her independence and freedom as an ordinary mill hand, embracing an uncertain future where she can nevertheless make her own decisions and choose her own partners. Thrown out by her mother, the final scene shows her, suitcase in hand, walking away down the street. 'Don't worry, lad,' she tells an enquiring neighbour, 'I'm a Lancashire lass and so long as there are spinning mills in Lancashire I can earn enough to keep myself respectable.' A final coda emphasises the cyclical nature of life, repeating the general scenes of the start of a typical day in Lancashire that we saw in the opening of the film. We see Fanny happily at work at the spinning machines – a handsome young factory hand asks her out to 'the pictures' and she cheerfully assents. As I've suggested, *Hindle Wakes* might be understood to represent the transition between early and late 1920s British filmmaking. Its experienced director, its stage source and the conservative directorial style of its second half seemed to look to the past, while the innovative camerawork and location shooting in its first half, its progressive social commentary and its deft visual symbolism looked towards the future.

The final film to be discussed in this chapter also has a modern industrial setting – that of the British film industry itself. In contrast to *Hindle Wakes*, *Shooting Stars* (A. V. Bramble & Anthony Asquith, 1928), is often discussed as a resolutely forward-looking, modern departure in British filmmaking. The film was made by British Instructional Pictures, which had established a strong reputation for documentary and instructional filmmaking since its founding in 1919. In particular, its series of First World War battle reconstruction films, such as *Ypres* (Walter Summers, 1925) and *The Battles of Coronel and Falkland Islands* (Walter Summers, 1927) provided British audiences a combination of documentary instruction, fictional re-enactment and remembrance ceremonial which was widely praised in the British press – the films were understood to be in a 'class apart' from the more frivolous narrative and romance driven accounts of the war coming from Hollywood studios (see Napper 2015: 33). *Shooting Stars* represented a new departure for the studio – an expansion into fiction film making which was perhaps a response to the recent passing of the Cinematograph Act. For its writer and director, it was definitely a new departure. Anthony Asquith was only 26 years old when the film was made, and it was his first attempt at directing – a fact the studio acknowledged by assigning the more experienced Bramble to work alongside him. Nevertheless, *Shooting Stars* is unmistakably Asquith's film and with his later (and equally celebrated) silent films *Underground* (1928) and *A Cottage on Dartmoor* (1929), it shares the sense of a young enthusiastic director *experimenting* with the medium – trying out different tricks and techniques of storytelling, shot construction and editing. In particular Asquith strives to convey information visually – dispensing as far as possible with inter-titles, and instead using symbolism, association and the exchange of narratively-charged objects to push his story along. Asquith had an intellectual approach to filmmaking – he was a member of the Film Society, and was often slightingly referred to as a 'highbrow' director in the trade press. He had voraciously devoured the films from Germany and Russia that where available to see in England, but he had also travelled to America, and was a particular fan of Chaplin and Lubitsch (see Miller 2016: 16). But despite his 'intellectual' reputation, he also had a keen sense of the melodramatic, and all three of his silent films are fundamentally dramas about desire and jealousy.

Shooting Stars opens with a filmmaking illusion. Mae Feather (Annette Benson) is perched in a tree laden with apple blossom. She has Mary Pickford-style ringlets, and is kissing Julian Gordon (Brian Ahern) who, dressed in cowboy shirt and hat, is evidently astride a horse. The camera pulls back briefly to give us a wider view as Julian rides away, and then closes back in on Mae who is now fondling a dove. She kisses it, but its beak pierces her lip and suddenly enraged she flings it away from her, no longer an innocent western heroine, but a frustrated and difficult film star. The illusion destroyed, we see Mae's point of view – the camera on its wheeled platform (or 'dolly') along with the director and the cameraman, and two studio hands on either side, still manually rolling the 'dolly' back. All of them are gazing upwards at the dove, which flutters in the rafters of the cavernous studio. The shot is ruined. Julian dismounts his wooden hobby horse, while various technicians attempt to retrieve the bird. The discrepancy between the onscreen world of beauty and glamour and the tiresome labour of actual film production in the ersatz 'calico world' of the studio is firmly established. Mae herself is the absolute embodiment of this discrepancy. 'I must say, Julian, your wife's a bit trying', the director tells her co-star. Noticing the set pianist's mood music for the scene has been 'Ain't She Sweet', he scratches his head, quizzically. An extraordinary crane shot now delineates the entire studio, following Mae as she wanders from the set she's just been working on (already being dismantled) up to a mezzanine level where another film, a slapstick comedy starring Andy Wilks (Donald Calthrop), is being made. Shot in the actual Cricklewood Studios owned (and rented to BIF) by Stoll, this scene gives a brilliant impression of the clutter and chaos of filmmaking in the period – the lighting rigs, the forest of scenery ropes and electricity cable, numerous filmmaking personnel, the musicians providing mood music. Watching Andy's scene being filmed is a gossip columnist from one of the fan magazines. 'I do love Andy Wilks, don't you?', she asks Mae, giving a hint of the plot to come. Later that hint is confirmed, when Mae gives the journalist an interview in her dressing room. Mae's responses to the clichéd questions she asks are conveyed by the notes she makes – 'Art... Poetry... Music... Pictures... Roses... Sunsets... Shakespeare... Children' are all carefully written down as Mae waxes lyrical. Her claim to 'adore all furred and feathered things' is undermined with a cut away to the studio hands joshing with each other outside her dressing room door. Having retrieved the hapless dove of the opening shot, they have fashioned it a cardboard Victoria Cross, which they hang around its neck: 'For Valour'.

Back in the dressing room, Julian puts his arms around Mae as they both smile ingratiatingly at the journalist, who accordingly notes down on

Fig. 15: *Shooting Stars* (1928); Mae (Annette Benson) and Julian (Brian Aherne) pretend to be the perfect couple.

her pad that Mae 'has found ideal mate'. But again, the film undercuts the lie. It cuts straight from the notepad to a shot of Andy Wilks at his dressing room mirror, confirming the suspicion set up in the earlier exchange – Andy is Mae's 'ideal mate', not Julian.

The incredible deftness and imagination of the visual storytelling evident in this opening sequence is maintained throughout the film, which remains inventive, even in the rare moments when it is heavy handed (at one point Andy extracts a coin from his pocket and touches Mae's temple with it – a rather laborious bit of business where a simple inter-title asking 'A penny for your thoughts?' would have sufficed). The plot itself revolves around the international ambitions of the stars. Andy has a contract to go to Hollywood, and Mae wishes to follow him. Julian, having discovered their affair, points out the clause in her Hollywood contract that requires her not to 'involve herself in any proceedings or actions of a scandalous nature liable to embarrass the management or damage her reputation in the eyes of the public'; it is the clause that became standard after the star scandals of the early 1920s (such as that of Fatty Arbuckle). Divorcing Julian would ruin her career, and since he indicates that he is not prepared to cover up her adultery, Mae must find another way to silence him. Throughout the film Asquith plays with different filmmaking styles – he even manages to incorporate a parody of a 'last minute rescue' film, a movie starring Mae and Julian which Julian sneaks into while Mae is spending the night with Andy, and is as excited and thrilled by as the little boys sitting behind him. At the climax of the film – the shooting incident itself – Asquith even incorporates some purely abstract imagery to convey the inner workings of his character's mind under extreme psychological pressure, a technique he would use again in *A Cottage on Dartmoor*.

Iris Barry's advice, to 'look two ways and move in neither, remaining British', was heeded, one might argue, by a number of the filmmakers discussed in this chapter. Certainly, by the late 1920s, British filmmakers were incorporating the styles and techniques developed by the Americans, the Germans and the Russians. But the internationalism of this cinema went beyond simply influences in film technique. Both Annette Benson and Estelle Brody were actually American stars, who had been brought over to work in British films in the hope that they might help sell them internationally. As we have seen, Florence Turner also came to work in the UK from America, and continued to work in both countries for many years. British actors and directors such as Guy Newell, Graham Cutts and Alfred Hitchcock all made films in both Germany and Britain, and by the end of the 1920s formal co-production agreements meant that European directors also came to Britain on multiple picture deals. The Hungarian Géza von Bolváry, having made the 'British' film *The Ghost Train* (1927) starring Guy Newell in Germany, came to Britain itself to make a series of films including *The Wrecker* (1929) and *The Vagabond Queen* (1929) (see Napper 2008: 38). E. A. Dupont, another big name in Germany after his critically acclaimed *Varieté* (1925) made a much publicised trip to the UK to make several films, including *Piccadilly* (1929), starring the Australian Gilda Grey and the Chinese-American Anna May Wong in a story set in a London nightclub (see Bergfelder 2008: 24). If Paul Rotha was disappointed not to find any truly 'national' tendencies in British films of the 1920s, perhaps that was because the industry was already too thrillingly cosmopolitan, and its workers citizens of the world.

Note

1   See also L. Napper (2009) *The British Cinema and Middlebrow Culture in the Interwar Years*. Exeter, Exeter University Press, 57–71.

CONCLUSION

Things have certainly moved on since Norma Desmond was mouldering away in her massive Hollywood mansion having been 'given the go-by' by a public which had no more use for silent cinema or its iconic stars. Who could have imagined in 1950 when *Sunset Boulevard* was made, that over sixty years later a silent film would once again dominate the Academy Awards ceremony, winning five major awards including Best Picture, as *The Artist* (Michel Hazanavicius, 2011) did in 2012? The critical and commercial success of *The Artist* (with its explicit tribute to the film-makers of the silent era) has accelerated a revival of interest in silent cinema, which was already well under way. Major long-running silent film festivals are held annually across the globe – notably in Pordenone, San Francisco, Bonn, Leicester and Bologna – as well as smaller events which nevertheless attract international attention, such as the silent film festival in the tiny town of Bo'ness in Scotland. Numerous local clubs hold regular screenings, offering the chance for audiences to experience silent film with live musical accompaniment, whether that be in rooms above pubs, in museums or in local cinemas. This book seeks to offer an introduction to readers new to the form, providing historical and theoretical context to some famous and not-so-famous examples from four filmmaking nations. Regrettably I've been unable to cover the rich histories of filmmaking in countries other than my chosen case studies. Sweden, France and Japan all produced impressive bodies of films in the 1920s and these are just the tip of the iceberg. As Norma Desmond says in the hit song from Andrew Lloyd Webber's musical version of her story, there's 'a world to rediscover...'

SELECT BIBLIOGRAPHY

Abel, R. (1999) *The Red Rooster Scare: Making Cinema American, 1900–1910.* Berkley: University of California Press.

Agate, J. (1930) 'The Film Till Now' in *The Tatler.* reprinted in J. Agate (1946) *Around Cinemas.* London: Home and Van Thal, 80.

Anon. (1919a) *Kinematograph Weekly,* 1 May, 67

____ (1919b) *Kinematograph* Weekly, 15 May, 89.

____ (1921) 'Fog Stops Kinema Shows', *Kinematograph Weekly,* 1 December.

____ (1927) *Hansard: Parliamentary Debates (Commons),* 16 March.

Barr, C. (2003) 'Before *Blackmail*: Silent British Cinema', in R. Murphy (ed.) *The British Cinema Book,* second edn. London: British Film Institute, 11–19.

____ (forthcoming) '"Don't Mention the War": The Soviet re-editing of *Three Live Ghosts*', in C. O'Sullivan and J. Cornu (eds) *The Translation of Films, from the 1900s to the 1940s.* Oxford: Oxford University Press.

Barr, C. and A. Kerzoncuf (2015) *Hitchcock Lost and Found.* Lexington: University of Kentucky Press.

Barry, I. (1924) 'A National or International Cinema?', *The Bioscope,* 28 February, 29.

Bergfelder, T. (2008) 'Life is a Variety Theatre: E. A. Dupont's Career in German and British Cinema', in T. Bergfelder and C. Cargnelli (eds) *Destination London: German-Speaking Emigrés and British Cinema, 1925–1930.* Oxford: Berghahn, 24–35.

Bordwell, D. (1988) 'An excessively obvious cinema', in D. Bordwell, J. Staiger and K. Thompson, *Classical Hollywood Cinema: Film Style and Mode of Production to 1960.* London: Routledge, 3–11.

_____ (2003) 'Monumental Heroics: Form and style in Eisenstein's silent films', in L. Grieveson and P. Kramer (eds) *The Silent Cinema Reader*. London: Routledge, 368–88.

_____ (2005) *Figures Traced in Light: On Cinematic Staging*. Berkley, CA: University of California Press.

Bryan, J. (2006) '"The cinema looking glass": The British film fan magazine, 1911–1918' (unpublished PhD thesis). Norwich: University of East Anglia.

Burrows, J. (2001) '"Our English Mary Pickford": Alma Taylor and ambivalent British stardom in the 1910s' in B. Babington (ed.) *British Stars and Stardom from Alma Taylor to Sean Connery* Manchester: Manchester University Press, 29–41.

_____ (2003) 'Big Studio Production in the Pre-quota Years', in R. Murphy (ed.) *The British Cinema Book*. London: British Film Institute, 20–7.

Crafton, D. (1999) *The Talkies: American Cinema's Transition to Sound 1926– 1931*. Berkley, CA: University of California Press.

Elsaesser, T. (2000) *Weimar Cinema and After: Germany's Historical Imaginary*. London: Routledge.

Fischer, L. (2009) 'Movies and the 1920s', in L. Fischer (ed.) *American Cinema of the 1920s: Themes and Variations*. New Brunswick, NJ: Rutgers University Press, 1–22.

Gaines, J. (2002) 'Of Cabbages and Authors' in J. Bean and D. Negra (eds) *A Feminist Reader in Early Cinema*. Durham & London: Duke University Press, 88–118.

Garncarz, J. (2003) 'Art and Industry: German cinema of the 1920s' in L. Grieveson and P. Kramer (eds) *The Silent Cinema Reader*. London: Routledge, 389–400.

Gledhill, C. (2003) *Reframing British Cinema 1918–1928: Between Restraint and Passion*. London: British Film Institute.

_____ (2007) 'Pastoral Transformations in 1920s British Cinema', in L. Porter and B. Dixon (eds) *Picture Perfect: Landscape, Place and Travel in British Cinema Before 1930*. Exeter: The Exeter Press, 37–47.

_____ (2015) 'Lydia Elizabeth Hayward (1879–1945)' in J. Nelmes and J. Selbo (eds) *Women Screenwriters: An International Guide*. New York: Springer.

Graffy, J. (2001) *Bed and Sofa*. London: IB Tauris.

Gunning, T. (1990) 'Weaving a Narrative: Style and Economic Background in Griffith's Biograph Films', in T. Elsaesser (ed.) *Early Cinema: Space, Frame, Narrative*. London: British Film Institute, 336–47.

____ (1991) 'Heard Over the Phone: *The Lonely Villa* and the de Lorde tradition of the terrors of technology', *Screen*, 32, 2, 184–95.

____ (2003) 'From the opium den to the theatre of morality: Moral discourse and the film process in early American cinema', in L. Grieveson and P. Kramer (eds) *The Silent Cinema Reader*. London: Routledge, 145–54.

Hake, S. (1992) *Passions and Deceptions: The Early Films of Ernst Lubitsch*. Princeton: Princeton University Press.

____ (2002) *German National Cinema*. London: Routledge.

Hales, B. (1996) 'Woman as Sexual Criminal: Weimar Constructions of the Criminal Femme Fatale', in *Women in German Yearbook*, 12, 101–21.

Higham, C. (2004) *Murder in Hollywood: Solving a Silent Screen Mystery*. Madison, WI: University of Wisconsin Press.

Higson, A. (1995) *Waving the Flag: Constructing a National Cinema in Britain*. Oxford: Clarendon Press.

____ (2002) *Young and Innocent: The Cinema in Britain 1896–1930*. Exeter: Exeter University Press.

Hutchinson, P. (2017) *Pandora's Box*. London: British Film Institute/Palgrave.

Kaes, A. (2009) *Shell Shock Cinema: Weimar Culture and the Wounds of War*. Princeton, NJ: Princeton University Press.

Kennedy, D. (1996) 'The New Drama and the New Audience' in M.R. Booth and J.H. Kaplan (eds) *The Edwardian Theatre: Essays on Performance and the Stage*. Cambridge: Cambridge University Press, 130–147.

Kepley, Jr, V. (1991) 'The origins of Soviet cinema: a study in industry development', in R. Taylor and I. Christie (eds) *Inside the Film Factory: New Approaches to Russian and Soviet Cinema*. London: Routledge, 60–79.

Koszarski, R. (1994) *An Evening's Entertainment: The Age of the Silent Feature Picture, 1915–1925*. Berkley, CA: University of California Press.

Kracauer, S. (1947) *From Caligari to Hitler: A Psychological History of the German Film*. Princeton, NJ: Princeton University Press.

____ (1995) *The Mass Ornament*, trans. and ed. T. Y. Levin. Cambridge, MA: Harvard University Press.

Low, R. (1971) *The History of the British Film 1918–1929*. London: George Allen & Unwin Ltd.

Maland, C. (2003) 'A star is born: American culture and the dynamics of Charlie Chaplin's star image, 1913–1916', in L. Grieveson and P. Kramer (eds) *The Silent Cinema Reader*. London: Routledge, 197–209.

Miller, H. (2016) 'What Price Cricklewood', in *Shooting Stars DVD Booklet*. London: British Film Institute DVD.

Miyao, D. (2007) *Sessue Hayakawa: Silent Cinema and Transnational Stardom*. Durham: Duke University Press.

Napper, L. (2008) 'Geza von Bolvary, Arnold Ridly and "Film Europe"', in T. Bergfelder and C. Cargnelli (eds) *Destination London: German-Speaking Emigrés and British Cinema, 1925–1930*. Oxford: Berghahn, 36–46.

____ (2009) *British Cinema and Middlebrow Culture in the Interwar Years*. Exeter: Exeter University Press

____ (2015) *The Great War in Popular British Cinema of the 1920s: Before Journey's End*. London: Palgrave.

O'Rourke, C. (2017) *Acting for the Silent Screen: Film Actors and Aspiration between the Wars*. London: I.B. Tauris.

Orgeron, M. (2003) 'Making It in Hollywood: Clara Bow, Fandom and Consumer Culture', *Cinema Journal*, 42, 4, 76–97.

Popple, S. and J. Kember (2003) *Early Cinema: from Factory Gate to Dream Palace*. London: Wallflower Press.

Reich, J. (2015) *The Maciste Films of Italian Silent Cinema*. Bloomington, IN: Indiana University Press.

Roberts, I. (2008) *German Expressionist Cinema: The World of Light and Shadow*. London: Wallflower Press.

Robinson, D. (1997) *Das Cabinet Des Dr. Caligari*. London: British Film Institute.

Rotha, P. (1967 [1930]) *The Film Till Now: A Survey of World Cinema*. London: Spring Books.

Sanders, L. (2002) '"Indecent Incentives to Vice": Regulating Films and Audience Behaviour from the 1890s to the 1910s' in A. Higson (ed.) *Young and Innocent: The Cinema in Britain 1896–1930*. Exeter: Exeter University Press, 97–110.

Sargeant, A. (2002) 'Popular Modernism: The Case of *Hindle Wakes*', *Film Studies*, 3, 47–58.

Saunders, T. J. (1994) *Hollywood in Berlin: American Cinema and Weimar Germany*. University of California Press.

Singer, B. (2003) 'Manhatten Nickelodeons: New data on audiences and exhibitors', in L. Grieveson and P. Kramer *The Silent Cinema Reader*. London: Routledge, 119–34.

Staiger, J. (1988) 'The central producer system after 1914', in D. Bordwell, J. Staiger and K. Thompson, *The Classical Hollywood Cinema: Film Style and Mode of Production to 1960*. London: Routledge, 128–41.

Stamp, S. (2015) *Lois Weber in Early Hollywood*. Berkley, CA: University of California Press.

Stead, L. (forthcoming) 'Dear Cinema Girls: Girlhood, Picturegoing and the Interwar Film Magazine' in C. Clay, M. DiCenzo, B. Green, F. Hackney (eds), *Women's Periodicals and Print Culture in Britain, 1918–1939: The Interwar Period*. Edinburgh: Edinburgh University Press.

Studlar, G. (1996) *This Mad Masquerade: Stardom and Masculinity in the Jazz Age*. New York: Columbia University Press.

____ (1999) 'The Perils of Pleasure? Fan Magazine Discourse as Women's Commodified Culture in the 1920s', in R. Abel (ed.) *Silent Film*. London: Athlone Press, 262–95.

Taylor, R. (1988) 'Soviet Cinema as Popular Culture: Or the Extraordinary Adventures of Mr Nepman in the Land of the Silver Screen', in *Revolutionary Russia*, 1, 1, 35–56.

Tsivian, Y. (1996) 'The Wise and Wicked Game: re-editing and Soviet film culture of the 1920s', *Film History*, 8, 3, 327–43.

____ (2000) Commentary to *Strike*. Eureka DVD.

____ (2002) Commentary to *Mad Love: Three Films by Evgenii Bauer*. British Film Institute DVD.

____ (2003) 'New notes on Russian film culture between 1908 and 1919', in L. Grieveson and P. Kramer (eds) *The Silent Cinema Reader*. London: Routledge, 339–348.

Vertov, D. (1992) *Kino-Eye: The Writings of Dziga Vertov*. Berkley, CA: University of California Press.

Williams, M. (2003) *Ivor Novello: Screen Idol*. London: British Film Institute.

Woolf, V. (1926) 'The Cinema', *The Nation and Athanaeum*, 3 July, 382.

Yampolsky, M. (1991) 'Kuleshov's experiments and the new anthropology of the actor', in R. Taylor and I. Christie (eds) *Inside the Film Factory: New Approaches to Russian and Soviet Cinema*. London: Routledge, 31–50.

Youngblood, D. J. (1992) *Movies for the Masses: Popular Cinema and Soviet Society in the 1920s*. Cambridge: Cambridge University Press.

____ (1999) *The Magic Mirror: Moviemaking in Russia, 1908–1918*. Madison: University of Wisconsin Press.

INDEX